Ghosts and Golems

Ghosts and Golems

Haunting Tales of the Supernatural

Compiled by Malka Penn

Illustrations by Theodor Black

The Jewish Publication Society
Philadelphia
2003 · 5763

Collection © 2001 Michele Palmer
Illustrations © Theodor Black

The Ghost of Leah Levy © 2001 Rivka Widerman
Wings © 2001 Deborah Spector Siegel
L'Dor V'Dor © 2001 Lois Ruby
The Ghost Well © 2001Ann Manheimer
Forgive Me © 2001 Jerry Raik
Mrs. Samson Is Upstairs © 2001 Susan Stone
The Shadow of the Golem © 2001 Michele Palmer
Jerusalem Tunnel © 2001 Hanna Bandes Geshelin
Hanukkah Light © 2001 Janni Lee Simner
My Grandma's Ghost © 2001 Carol Snyder

Paperback edition 2003.
The Jewish Publication Society
2100 Arch Street
Philadelphia, PA 19103

Design and composition by Sandy Freeman
Manufactured in the United States of America

03 04 05 06 07 08 09 10 10 9 8 7 6 5 4 3 2 1

Library of Congress Cataloging-in-Publication Data

Ghosts and golems : haunting tales of the supernatural / compiled by Malka Penn;
illustrations by Theodor Black.
    p. c.m.
   Summary: A collection of ten original contemporary stories of the supernatural which
reflect a Jewish tradition that can be traced to the biblical story of Saul and the spirit of
Samuel.
   ISBN 0-8276-0733-4
   1. Children's stories, Jewish. [1. Supernatural—Fiction. 2. Ghosts—Fiction. 3. Short
stories.] I. Penn, Malka. II. Black, Theodor, ill.
PZ5 .G343 2001
[Fic]—dc21

                                          2001029682

Contents

Introduction

Jewish stories of the supernatural belong to an ancient tradition. The very first Jewish ghost story, in fact, appears in the Bible, when Saul asks the Witch of Endor to invoke the spirit, or ghost, of Samuel. Since then, countless Jewish folktales and legends of ghosts, demons, golems, and other supernatural beings have been recounted and handed down from generation to generation.

The tales in this collection are part of that tradition with one important difference: they are original stories, with contemporary children as the main characters. Like all good ghost stories, they are suspenseful and haunting. Because they are also Jewish, they are sometimes humorous, and often thought-provoking. Many of them explore the nature of loss, through the ghost of a grandparent or other loved one.

Of course, the stories are as varied as their authors. They range in settings from the American West to Israel. They touch on personal turning points like Bat Mitzvahs and family changes. They confront issues of loneliness, identity, and forgiveness.

As the young people in these stories deal with external apparitions, they begin to resolve their own internal concerns and conflicts. In the process, they gain a new understanding of themselves and the Jewish tradition.

Malka Penn

The Ghost of Leah Levy

~ Rivka Widerman ~

Aliza knew, even in the darkness of the porch, that she was not alone. "Who's there?" she asked.

No one answered. She felt a prickle on the back of her neck, the way she did when something made her uneasy, so quick she hardly noticed. She thought she could make out a figure, a silhouette of darker against dark standing next to her.

Must be some shadow play caused by the lightning, she thought. Or rather, wanted to think, for the lightning was too far away to affect the shadows where she sat.

Aliza focused her attention back on the coming storm, which had darkened the early afternoon sky. The blasts of thunder and flashes of lightning over the nearby buttes and eroding mountains were about all that she really enjoyed about being in Interior, South Dakota, population sixty-seven, the prairie town on the outskirts of Badlands National Park where she was to spend the summer. She did like the wildflowers, too, which were unusually abundant this year, but nothing captivated her like a heavy storm.

She stayed on the porch. Lightning was one of the great natural dangers of life in the Badlands and on the prairie. There were few trees; people stood taller than anything else and made an easy target. Although Aliza loved looking at storms, she never watched one while standing in the open.

"It's like God talking," she had told her parents when they had once asked why she liked watching the storms. "The way He did to the Israelites in the wilderness."

"Well, the Badlands certainly are a wilderness," her father had said.

"And a place of exile," Aliza had added angrily. "Why couldn't we stay in Vermont?"

"You know why, Aliza. Your mother and I received a grant for the summer to research black-footed ferrets, and, they, as you know, do not inhabit Vermont."

"Why this summer, the summer before my Bat Mitzvah? I should be back home getting ready for it with all my friends."

Her parents had not responded. Since Aliza had arrived in Interior, she had made no friends. There were few children, and even fewer, especially Jewish ones, with whom Aliza thought she could share the excitement and anticipation of her upcoming Bat Mitzvah, the synagogue ceremony in which she would pass from child to adult, when she would read from the Torah in front of the entire congregation and then have a huge party with music, games, speeches by her parents and teachers saying how wonderful she was, ice cream, new clothes. Calling and e-mailing her friends back home didn't provide much consolation.

Aliza's Bat Mitzvah portion was to be chapters 29:9–30 of Deuteronomy, the section called Nitsavim in Hebrew, where Moses tells Israel of the blessings God has in store for them if they follow His commandments and the curses if they don't. She had been on the porch studying one of its verses—". . . life and death I place before you, blessing and curse; now choose life so that you may live . . ."—when she realized that the storm was coming in from the north.

"That was one choice I didn't get to make when my parents decided to come to this dead town," she mumbled as she closed her book.

The storm moved closer. Aliza could see patches of nearby grassland in the flashes of lightning. Soon the storm would advance enough to illuminate the porch. She watched and waited and listened for the thunder. The lightning was quick, but not so quick that Aliza could not see that someone was indeed standing next to her. A girl. A girl with long, dark braids, wearing ankle-high boots and a striped apron or pinafore over a dark dress. Aliza could almost touch her. At the next flash of lightning an instant later, the girl was gone.

Aliza, though she thought she knew better, could have sworn that she had just seen a ghost. No one in Interior dressed in clothes so old-fashioned or wore her hair like that. She thought of her own flaming red hair cut short on the sides and back to keep her neck cool in the summer heat.

If she were a ghost, I'd be afraid, Aliza said to herself. But Aliza did not think that she had been afraid. She thought of how solid the girl had seemed, not at all like the wispy, transparent things that ghosts were supposed to be.

Aliza considered what else she knew about ghosts and realized that it wasn't much. Most of what she knew she had learned from books or movies. This ghost didn't seem like any of those ghosts. She hadn't rattled chains or howled in the night. In fact, when she appeared it had been in the light of lightning, not in the dark. The rest of Aliza's knowledge about ghosts came from stories told long ago by her grandfather, which were mostly about Jewish ghosts. They came only in dreams, Aliza remembered him saying. Aliza had been wide awake. And the girl hadn't seemed scary. Aliza was sure that she had felt more comfort than dread.

I must have imagined it, she decided. That's what comes from all these days of having no one to talk to. I'll tell Mom and Dad that I'm so sick with loneliness I'm starting to hallucinate.

But Aliza didn't say anything to her parents about her possibly ghostly vision. Later that afternoon, after the storm had blown past and the sun had brightened the sky again, Aliza and her parents sat down to an early dinner.

"Aliza," her mother said as she dished out the food. "Your father and I have something to tell you."

Her mother's voice held a cheery note, but Aliza was wary. Good news never followed this sort of beginning,

"Our grant has been extended. We'll be staying in Interior through the fall and winter."

"We'll go home for my Bat Mitzvah, right?" Aliza asked hopefully.

Her mother looked at Aliza's father. "To get more grant money, we had to expand our research; our schedule is really tight. We thought that you could have your Bat Mitzvah in Rapid City. It's only about an hour by car from here. The party—"

"NO!" Aliza cried. "Rapid City is hours by plane from anyone I care about. If I can't have my Bat Mitzvah along with all my friends, then I don't want one at all."

"Aliza, dear," her mother began, but Aliza interrupted her. "Who cares about ferrets, anyway? They're mean, just like you."

Before her mother or father could say anything more, Aliza jumped up from the table and stormed out of the house. She walked past the Badlands Gas Station, the Interior Laundromat, the Badlands General Store, and the Wooden Arrow Cafe. She did not really see any of these. She did not notice the shortgrass prairie rippling like the waves of the sea in the breeze, or the Badlands rising like a wall to stop the prairie's flow, or the clouds rolling on endlessly in the blue sky. She was aware only of being the loneliest, most miserable girl on the prairie.

"All they think about are endangered species," Aliza muttered as she walked. "Don't they know that twelve-year-old girls are an endangered species in this place?"

Having passed most of Interior's landmarks, Aliza soon found herself at the cemetery. The sadness of the place, with its rusty metal gate and graves overgrown with buffalo grass and yellow clover, fit her mood and she went in. Aliza had met everyone in town but recognized no names as she walked among the gravestones. William P. Smith had died at age nineteen in the last month of World War I; George Dienster at age twenty-one in Vietnam. The McCourt family had lost a set of infant twins in the 1920s—twice.

Aliza was drawn to a grave that lay alone in the corner of the cemetery. I bet it's another set of McCourt twins, she thought as she made her way over to see it. But it wasn't. The small flat stone that marked the grave read:

LEAH LEVY
1898–1910, 5658–5670

Aliza read the gravestone several times. Each time it read "Leah Levy." She read it aloud. She heard herself say "Leah Levy."

Wouldn't you just know it. The only other Jewish girl in this town, and she's dead, Aliza frowned. She was only twelve when she died. The same age as I am. I wonder if she made it to her Bat Mitzvah.

Aliza spoke to Leah Levy's gravestone. "Were you the only Jewish girl in Interior? All my friends are back home. They're all studying for their Bat Mitzvahs and planning their parties. No one here knows what a Bat Mitzvah is. Except my parents. And they don't care about mine. Do you know what a Bat Mitzvah is? Girls didn't always have them. It's like a Bar Mitzvah for a boy. It means that you're grown up and . . ." Aliza paused. The girl that lay at her feet might have died before she had ever known of parties and Torah portions. "You must think that I'm selfish and silly."

Aliza looked around for a few stones to place on Leah Levy's grave— the Jewish way of marking a visit to a graveside, which she had learned from visits to her grandmother's grave with her parents.

"I hope you died peacefully, Leah Levy," she said. At that moment, she felt the skin on the back of her neck prickle for a second. She thought she saw a girl with long dark braids, ankle-high boots, and a striped pinafore over a dark dress. She was standing next to the gravestone, her hand outstretched as if reaching for something.

The same girl she had seen in the lightning flash earlier in the day.

"Talk to me, please," Aliza shouted. But the girl didn't. She just vanished.

Was it the ghost of Leah Levy? Aliza wondered. She made up her mind then and there that the next time she saw the girl with the long dark braids she would catch her, ghost or not.

To catch the ghost of Leah Levy, Aliza understood that she needed to know more about Leah Levy herself. She went straight to the one person in Interior she thought might know something: Mrs. Verde, part owner of the Wooden Arrow Cafe and, more important, the president of the Interior Historical Society. If anyone knew anything about Leah Levy, she would.

"Hello, Aliza," Mrs. Verde said as Aliza shut the café door behind her. "Can I get you anything?"

"Hello, Mrs. Verde. Thanks, but I don't want anything to eat," Aliza replied. "Can I ask you a question? It's about the cemetery."

"The cemetery? Sure. Go ahead."

"You know that little grave in a corner, the one that belongs to Leah Levy?"

"Yes. The Levys opened the first store in Interior in 1908. Leah was their only daughter."

"Do you know how she died?"

"No, I don't. I do know that there was no Jewish cemetery in Interior, so they gave her a little corner all her own. You know, Aliza, I think the Levys may have been the only Jewish people in Interior until you and your family arrived."

Leah Levy was just like her, Aliza thought. Young, Jewish, and alone. "Thank you, Mrs. Verde," she said as she left. "Thank you very much."

The next day Aliza returned to the cemetery. She placed a few more stones on Leah Levy's grave and waited, but she saw no one and nothing except the breeze waving the grass in the bright sunlight. She came the day after that and the day after that. Each time she placed another stone on Leah Levy's grave. Each time she was alone.

Aliza began to believe that she would never see the girl again. Still, she came to the cemetery. To while away the time, she studied the wildflowers and grasses that grew on and around the graves. She had plenty of time; she had stopped studying for her Bat Mitzvah.

One day, as she bent over to examine a patch of buffalo grass growing over Leah Levy's grave, she heard a high-pitched voice say, "I don't care much for grass. I like flowers better, don't you?" Aliza, startled, spun around and saw a girl standing behind her, a girl with long dark braids who was wearing an old-fashioned pinafore.

Before Aliza could reply, the girl continued. "I could show you some beautiful flowers. Meet me tomorrow on the Medicine Root Trail." Then, just as she had the last time, the girl vanished.

Aliza was shaken at first by the girl's appearance. Her neck prickled with an uneasiness at something she couldn't name. But when Aliza thought about what the girl had said, her uneasiness vanished in an instant, just like the girl had, and turned into elation. "She asked me to meet her. Tomorrow. I can't wait," Aliza almost shouted with joy.

The next day, the weather was cool and dry. Aliza asked her mother to drop her off at the ranger's station. From there she made her way to the Medicine Root Trail. The spring and summer had been wetter than in years past, and the usually arid grasslands bordering the Badlands were lush with wildflowers.

She walked slowly, stopping every few steps to have a better look at one flower or another. The trail narrowed and almost disappeared under the knee-high needle-and-thread grass that had encroached upon it. Aliza stopped to pick off the needlelike blades that had stuck to her shins. In the meadow to the right of the trail she saw a girl—the girl!

The girl seemed engrossed in a showy milkweed. "Don't you think that this is the most beautiful flower on the prairie?" she said at last. "I love how you can see the buds and blooms all at the same time. It's such a nice pink. I wanted a dress in that color. There was some showy milkweed growing by the side of our store, but my mother pulled it out. She planted a rosebush. Have you seen it? Our store, I mean. The rosebush didn't do too well. Our store is on the main street."

"Who are you?" Aliza already knew the answer, but she needed to ask.

"Don't you know? We've met three times already."

She had to be! Still, she hesitated a moment before she said, "You're

Leah Levy."

The girl smiled and turned her attention back to the pink blossoms of the milkweed.

"The last time, at the cemetery—why did you ask me here?"

The girl looked puzzled. "I told you. I wanted to show you my favorite flowers," she said. "I wanted to see you."

Aliza was at a loss for words, but Leah Levy continued. "You came to visit me. You put stones on my grave. You called to me. No one has done that since my family left Interior.

"I've been alone since I died. My mother promised to come and place a stone on my grave every year, but she never did. Neither did my father. My brother visited me once, but he was a grown man by then. I barely recognized him. To be forgotten, that's been the worst of all.

"We were the only Jews for miles. And I was the only girl for miles, too. I only ever had one friend, a Sioux girl whose family came from the reservation to trade with my father. I didn't see her very often. Then she died. Of measles. So did my brother Sammy. Only my younger brother Jonah and I were left. He was too little to be a friend. So I just died of loneliness."

"How . . . ?" Aliza was afraid to finish the question.

"I was hit by lightning."

Aliza shuddered.

Leah Levy went on, "I was never lonely when I stood among the wildflowers. I was out here with Jonah when I saw lightning over the Badlands. It was very dry that year. I was sure the rain would come and make everything bloom instantly. I ran back to the house with Jonah and got him inside. Then I ran out again. I wanted to see the rain make the prairie bloom." Leah Levy paused. She looked straight into Aliza's eyes. "You must be lonely, too."

"Why do you say that?"

"Why else would you come every day to visit me?"

Aliza burst into tears. She told Leah Levy everything—about her family coming to Interior, her parents' research, her friends back home planning their Bat Mitzvahs, about having no one to talk to about anything. Leah Levy listened, and Aliza felt that at last there was at least one person she could talk to—even if that person might be a ghost.

The air that had been only a breeze began to pick up in speed. The meadowlarks that had perched quietly on the telephone wires began to chatter almost hysterically, flocking together, turning sharply and flying fast. In the distance, the sky over the Badlands had turned from blue to gray. There was a faint flash of lightning. A storm was heading their way.

"I should get back to the ranger station," Aliza said. "Before the storm gets here."

"The storm is far away," Leah Levy said. "Let's walk a little longer."

They walked together on the overgrown path, pausing occasionally to ponder some small purple flower or another showy milkweed. Aliza noticed that the lightning that had been so faint a short while before had become brighter and she could hear the low rumble of thunder. Aliza knew that she had to get to shelter before the lightning came close enough to hit her. But they had been walking away from the direction of the ranger station. If she did not head back there quickly, she would surely be caught in the storm.

"I have to go now," she said to Leah Levy. "The storm is getting too close."

"You still have time. The lightning is not yet near," Leah Levy said serenely.

"But we're too far from the ranger's station for me to make a quick dash when it gets here." Aliza was becoming frantic.

"Stay here with me," Leah Levy said softly.

"If I stay, I could die."

"If you go, you'll only be lonely again."

Aliza looked at Leah Levy as if seeing her for the first time. Before, she had only noticed the long dark braids and the old-fashioned clothing. Now she could see the ashenness of her face, so white it seemed never to have known a blush on the cheeks. Her eyes were black and vacant; no light reflected from her irises.

Aliza suddenly understood why Leah Levy had finally appeared to her that day. "You want me to be hit by lightning, just like you were. You want me to die so that you won't be alone."

"So that we won't be alone," Leah Levy said fiercely.

"I thought you were my friend. How could you ask such a thing? Friends don't ask each other to die."

"I am already dead. Choose me or choose to be lonely."

Lightning cracked again and the boom of thunder came almost instantly. Aliza knew the storm was very close.

"Choose," the thunder seemed to say. Choose what? To stay and let a bolt of lightning hit her so she would be with Leah Levy forever, or to leave, to run to the ranger's station and her lonely life? Aliza did not know what to do. Each time she heard the thunder clap, it shouted, "Choose, choose."

And then they came to her, through the lightning and the thunder, the words of her Bat Mitzvah portion, the ones she had been reading just before Leah Levy first appeared: "Life and death I place before you, blessing and curse; now choose life so that you may live."

Leah Levy stretched out her hand. "Wait with me. We'll never be lonely again."

"No!" Aliza screamed. She would not choose Leah Levy. Her loneliness would not kill her. She would go home one day soon, see her friends. If her family stayed in Interior, she would make new friends somehow. She would live.

She looked into Leah Levy's black, empty eyes. "I hate being lonely. I hate that you're lonely, but I won't die for you. Can't you see that?"

Leah Levy said nothing. Aliza could no longer wait. "I can't die to be your friend. But I promise you this, I will never forget you."

Aliza ran from Leah Levy's outstretched hand and toward the ranger station as fast as she could, stumbling twice but still running. When she reached the trailhead she turned around to catch her breath and check the progress of the storm. She saw Leah Levy in a flash of lightning, standing where she had left her, her hand still beckoning. She could hear her voice between the claps of thunder: "We'll never be lonely again. . . ."

~ Background Note from the Author ~

I wrote "The Ghost of Leah Levy" right after a trip I made to South Dakota. While there, I was struck by the loneliness, first of the landscape and then of Jews who were among the pioneers of the Dakota Territory. Ghosts also strike me as being lonely; they haunt the places of their lives, or deaths, not so much because they are unwilling to be dead as because they are unwilling to be alone in being dead. Loneliness can drive one to terrible actions or to brave ones. I wanted to explore these different kinds of loneliness in a story.

The story takes place in Interior, South Dakota, just outside the Badlands National Park. Interior and the park are real. I have fictionalized the names of stores, trails and their locations, and other landmarks. Aliza and her family are figments of my imagination; Mrs. Verde is based on a real person. The ghost, Leah Levy, is also fictional, but her story is gathered from historical accounts of Jews who settled in the Northern Plains. The sources I relied on most were Sophie Turpin's *Dakota Diaspora: Memoirs of a Jewish Homesteader,* published by the University of Nebraska Press in 1984; and Linda Mack Schloff's *"And Prairie Dogs Weren't Kosher": Jewish Women in the Upper Midwest since 1855,* published by the Minnesota Historical Society Press in 1996.

~ About the Author ~

RIVKA WIDERMAN loves to read ghost stories, but this is the first one she has written. She lives in New York City with her husband and reviews children's books for the Children's Book Committee at Bank Street College of Education.

Wings

~ Deborah Spector Siegel ~

Though it was one of those perfect summer days, bright and clear and not too hot, Sergey felt as if a stone had settled in the pit of his stomach. He was about to enter Grandma and Grandpa's house for the first time since Grandpa Abe had died two days ago. A crowd of mourners, including Sergey's Grandma, parents, and older brother, Ivan, had just returned from the burial to begin *shivah,* the seven days of Jewish mourning. Sergey's family, who lived in a distant suburb, was staying with Grandma for the entire week of *shivah.*

Now Sergey stood outside on the front lawn with his brother at the end of a long line of mourners, mostly old folks who had been lifelong friends of Grandma and Grandpa's. Each person had to wash his hands, wash away the uncleanness of the cemetery and death before entering the house. Sergey's parents had asked the boys to stay at the end of the line in case any of the mourners needed help. A large pitcher of water set in a wide bowl and a stack of towels had been placed on a small table at the bottom of the porch steps. Sergey watched the mourners pour water over their hands, then slowly climb the stairs before going inside the house for the first *shivah* meal. He wondered what his grandparents' house would feel like now with Grandpa Abe gone. Already the old house, looming up strangely before him, reminded Sergey of everything Grandpa Abe and he had done together— their walks to *shul,* the family gatherings and Sabbath dinners, and—most of all—the jokes they'd shared together. Grandpa Abe's mischievous smile and sense of humor had been legendary. As long as Sergey had known him, he had loved to tell jokes, make up funny words, and tell what he jokingly called *zayde meises*—the Grandpa tales, his takeoff on the Yiddish expression *bubbe meises*—the Grandma tales. Grandpa Abe, the rabbi had said in his eulogy, had been a man who loved making people laugh.

Sergey stood in line listening to the conversations of people around him, friends and neighbors who had known Grandpa Abe. Grandpa hadn't been in the least bit sick or frail but had died unexpectedly in his sleep, full of energy and life, at the age of eighty-four. People were saying how good it was that Abe had made it to such a ripe old age, as if dying that old wasn't such a big deal. But Grandpa hadn't seemed all that old to Sergey. He'd been lively, even boyish at times. "Ever since I got old, I'm getting younger and younger," Grandpa had joked to Sergey just last week. For the first time in Sergey's eleven years, he realized that death was like coming to the end of a long, wonderful book, long before you wanted it to end. "Our loved ones live on in the hearts and minds of those who cherish their memory," the rabbi had said at the funeral. Sergey wondered if that meant that remembering them was a way to somehow reread that book, to bring the person back to life.

As Sergey moved slowly behind his brother, he found himself remembering funny things Grandpa Abe had said over the years—things he hadn't thought about for a very long time. One memory in particular kept popping back into his mind. It was when he had been a small boy in this house and Grandpa used to pop up from behind his big overstuffed chair, startling Sergey and shouting one of his funny, strange made-up words. Sergey could still remember the feeling of being both thrilled and scared when Grandpa did that. But he couldn't quite remember the word, which seemed right on the tip of his tongue.

"Ivan?" Sergey asked. "Do you remember that long, funny word Grandpa Abe made up when we were little?"

"Not really," Ivan said, tapping his foot impatiently on the walkway. Sergey knew Ivan had loved Grandpa Abe as much as he did, but he could tell that Ivan would have preferred being back in his own room with his CD player and headphones on listening to heavy metal instead of staying over at Grandma's for seven long days of *shivah*. Even their mother, who had torn her blouse in grief that morning with Grandma, had said that observing *shivah* was hard. It forced people to envelop themselves completely in mourning.

"Don't you remember how Grandpa used to love making up funny words from Russian, Yiddish, and English syllables?" Sergey asked, a little annoyed at Ivan.

Ivan shrugged. "You mean *zayde meises*—the Grandpa tales he always told?"

"No, that long nonsense word he'd always scare us with," said Sergey.

"Scared you with maybe," Ivan said nonchalantly. "Those words didn't mean anything. They were just nonsense words made up from the languages he knew."

"But they were so funny and real-sounding," Sergey said. "Especially that one word he used to tease us with all the time when we were little."

Ivan rolled his eyes with the effort of remembering. "You're the one who still remembers the little kid stuff, not me."

"I think it started out 'hop,' then had a bunch of syllables, then ended in 'cuckoo.'" Sergey said, ignoring him.

In spite of himself, Ivan's eyes widened in a flash of sudden remembrance. "Oh . . . the cuckoo word! Hopchunurabasticuckoo!" Ivan rolled it off as easily as his own name.

"I thought you couldn't remember little kid stuff," Sergey teased.

"Well, that crazy word I do."

"Hop-chu-nura, what was it again, Ivan?" Sergey asked excitedly.

". . . basticuckoo," Ivan finished.

"Hop-chu-nura-basti-cuckoo," Sergey repeated slowly. "Hey, remember how Grandpa used to sneak up behind us and say it just to startle us? We'd scream and run away. It was sort of like a game of tag. Instead of saying you're It, Grandpa would jump out and call 'Hopchunurabasticuckoo!'"

"You're the one who screamed and ran away. You'd run crying to Grandma," Ivan said accusingly.

"Hopchunurabasticuckoo!" Sergey suddenly yelled near Ivan's ear, making him flinch.

"Shush, you boys! Please!" said an older lady Sergey recognized from Grandpa's *shul*. She had turned around in line and was staring at them. She looked shocked. Sergey and Ivan looked up at the line of mourners. Everyone was staring at them.

"Joking and merrymaking at such a time!" the lady chided them some more.

Ivan looked away, embarrassed.

"We were just remembering this really funny word Grandpa made up once," Sergey piped up in their defense.

"Let them joke," said an old man in front of Ivan. "Their *zayde* was a funny man. I remember he said to me once, 'I would get old, if only I could find the time.'"

Everyone chuckled. Soon people were chatting noisily, remembering Grandpa Abe and his sense of humor—and the moment of tension was broken.

"See?" the man turned to Ivan and patted his arm. "We all remember your Grandpa Abe's jokes. That's how we keep him alive. In here." The man tapped his head.

"I guess we better keep on saying 'Hopchunurabasticuckoo' then," Sergey whispered to Ivan with a mischievous smile.

"You remind me of Grandpa when you smile like that," Ivan said.

~

The line ahead of them moved up slowly. Several times the water ran out, and Ivan ran inside to refill the pitcher. Another time Sergey ran to help a latecomer out of a car, an elderly woman who had come to join the mourners. Finally all of the old folks had washed their hands and gone inside, leaving Ivan and Sergey alone in front of the house. While Ivan poured water over his own hands from the pitcher, Sergey walked to the edge of the lawn and glanced around to see if there were any other mourners arriving. He spotted one, a tall, elderly, stoop-shouldered man, coming hurriedly up the block, with a prayer book in his hand. It must be another one of Grandpa's friends from the *shul,* Sergey thought as he watched him approach. His stride was strangely familiar. The man turned and started up Grandma's walkway. Sergey felt the hair on the back of his neck stand completely on end. Almost involuntarily, he stepped several paces backward. It was all he could do to keep from crying out. It was Grandpa Abe himself, unmistakable in his shiny black *yarmulke* and the familiar gray sweater-vest he had always worn.

"Grandpa?" Sergey gasped out in astonishment.

Grandpa Abe had stopped in the middle of the walkway and seemed to be staring past Sergey toward the house, with a look of longing in his eyes. Then, as quickly as he had appeared, he just faded away.

Sergey's heart was beating like a pack of stampeding horses. He let out his breath in a long, low whistle. He'd obviously been hallucinating. How weird! He'd never before hallucinated in his life.

"Did you see that?" Sergey said, yanking on the back of Ivan's shirt.

"See what?" said Ivan, toweling off his hands.

"There, behind us."

Ivan turned around and stared at the empty walkway. "What was it?" Ivan said, laying the towel down.

"You didn't see anyone?" Sergey said.

"No. Who did you see?"

Sergey couldn't possibly blurt out that he'd just seen Grandpa Abe coming up the walk with his prayer book just like he was one of the mourners. Besides, his own mind was already telling him that it was probably one of those strange mental things that happened right after a funeral. He thought he'd seen something like it on *Unsolved Mysteries* once.

"Oh, nobody," Sergey said. "Just someone on the street I thought I recognized."

"Oh." Ivan shrugged, climbed the steps, and went in. Sergey hurriedly washed and dried his hands, resisting the almost overwhelming urge to turn around and look behind him, just in case Grandpa reappeared with that homesick look on his face. As nice as it had been to see Grandpa again, he wasn't sure he was up to another sighting on an empty stomach. He ran up the porch steps, threw open the front door, and quickly shut it behind him. He stood catching his breath and taking in the strangely cheerful hubbub of all the mourners and the fragrant smell of food. He was grateful for all the people who were there. It kept the place from seeming too desolate. Besides, he told himself, a person definitely wouldn't hallucinate in the middle of a noisy crowd.

In the dining room, people were putting out the first *shivah* meal, a huge spread that looked more like a feast than a funeral meal. Sergey's parents and Grandma and Grandpa's other daughter and son, who were also Sergey's aunt and uncle, were already eating. Grandma looked pale and alone even with all of the family around her, but at least she was eating a little. There were piles of fresh bagels and rye bread, bowls of cottage cheese, cream cheese with chives, hard-boiled eggs, herring in sour cream, tuna fish and applesauce—a dairy meal that represented life and new beginnings The rabbi had explained that even in the midst of grief you were supposed to be looking forward to life. Sergey loaded up his plate from the buffet. It was amazing how famished he was. He felt as if he'd been running for hours instead of sitting and standing around a funeral all day. Sergey decided right there at the buffet table that his vision of Grandpa Abe had been caused by extreme hunger.

There weren't enough chairs in the dining room, so Sergey and Ivan took their plates and wandered into the living room where the crowd had overflowed. Everyone sat oddly, on tiny little stools, or on Grandma's chairs and couches—but with all of the cushions removed. The younger people sat right on the floor. Sergey and Ivan had gone to a great-aunt's *shivah* once, and they knew that mourners were supposed to sit low to the ground, as near to the earth as possible, in sympathy with the deceased. The rabbi had said that *shivah* was not supposed to distract you from your sadness or cheer you up, but to make you feel your loss even more—so that after seven days of grieving, healing could begin.

Ivan and Sergey sat down on the carpeted floor, leaned against a wall, and lunged into their food. Sergey took a large bite out of a bagel-and-cream-cheese sandwich and nodded at Mr. Schwartz, an old friend of Grandpa's who was sitting nearby on a footstool and finishing his plate of food. Mr. Schwartz smiled at Sergey and Ivan. "I'm going for coffee now. Can I bring you boys anything?"

Sergey and Ivan shook their heads. "No thank you, Mr. Schwartz," Sergey said politely. Mr. Schwartz got up and wandered toward the dining room. Suddenly, a shadow fell as another man shuffled over to the stool and started to sit down in his place. Sergey glanced up to say that the stool was already taken by Mr. Schwartz, but the words stalled in his throat. The man was none other than Grandpa Abe! He had brought along an entire plate of eggs and a saltshaker, which he balanced on his lap. Sergey couldn't believe what happened next. Grandpa Abe sat right down and happily salted and ate one hard-boiled egg after another! Grandpa Abe had always loved hard-boiled eggs. Grandma used to warn him not to eat so many because they were so high in cholesterol. Now Grandpa Abe was brazenly eating his way through an entire plate filled with eggs!

"You shouldn't eat all those!" Sergey croaked in a shocked, strangled voice, as Grandpa chomped into his fourth egg. He didn't seem to hear or notice Sergey at all. He seemed in a happy egg-filled world of his own. Suddenly Sergey realized that Mr. Schwartz had returned and was slowly easing himself back down on the stool with a mug of hot coffee in one hand and a plate of coffee cake in the other. Sergey winced and squeezed his eyes shut, waiting for Mr. Schwartz to holler and spill his hot coffee when he sat down on Grandpa Abe and his hard-boiled eggs.

"Why not?" said Ivan, already scraping his plate. "I'm starved." Ivan thought Sergey had been talking to him.

"Huh?" Sergey said, opening his eyes. Grandpa and his plate of eggs were in the last stages of fading away. A second later, only Mr. Schwartz sat on the stool, unaware that he had sat down on Grandpa Abe. Mr. Schwartz took a sip of coffee and looked sympathetically at both boys. "I *davened* with your Grandpa at *shul* for many years, you know. He was a wonderful man. I'm going to miss that sense of humor of his."

"Me too," said Ivan, as Sergey just sat there with his mouth open. Ivan polished off his plate of food and stood up. "I'm going back for seconds, Serge. For some reason I have this incredible craving for hard-boiled eggs," he added.

~

The following days of *shivah* were the strangest Sergey had ever known. He had one weird sighting of Grandpa Abe after another. He would catch glimpses of him moving busily about the house as if he still had a purpose, opening drawers and rummaging around, or napping in his favorite overstuffed chair, oblivious to the mourners around him. One morning Sergey even spotted Grandpa Abe wrapping tefillin on his arm in the back bedroom, just as he had his whole life, to say the morning prayers. The visions were pleasant yet somehow disturbing to Sergey, as if, on his way to the Next World, Grandpa Abe kept forgetting things and had to keep stopping back at the house to retrieve them. Each time Sergey spotted him, he'd suck in his breath, close his eyes, and pretend he wasn't seeing what he was seeing. After a minute or two the vision would fade away, and Sergey could open his eyes with a sigh of relief. He was especially nervous that Grandma might stumble onto Grandpa Abe wandering around the house and collapse in shock.

On the sixth night of *shivah,* Sergey was lying in his sleeping bag next to Ivan on Grandma's living room floor, his hands behind his head, unable to sleep. Moonlight from an open curtain spilled across the floor. Sergey was deep in thought, wondering about his ongoing sightings of Grandpa. He was beginning to wonder if he had done something to cause these appearances of Grandpa Abe, since he seemed to be the only one who was seeing him.

It had all seemed to start right after the funeral, during hand washing when everyone was talking about Grandpa's famous sense of humor and he and Ivan had started up with that crazy word. Hopchunurabasticuckoo.

Suddenly Sergey felt that now-familiar prickly feeling on the back of his neck—and he knew it was happening again. Sure enough, a second later, Grandpa Abe appeared at the foot of his sleeping bag as if summoned, smiling that mischievous smile of his and looking way too lively for a dead person.

Sergey sat up with a gasp. For the first time since Grandpa had started making his strange appearances, Sergey felt an icy rush of fear, like a lone explorer on the edge of a scary frontier. As he had all week, Sergey closed his eyes and waited for Grandpa's image to fade away.

Slowly, he began to open his eyes, half squinting. But this time, Grandpa had not faded away. He seemed as wide-eyed and full of life as ever, though Sergey noticed for the first time that Grandpa's form was surrounded by a soft white glow, not unlike the whitish glow of the moon. Again, Grandpa didn't seem to look at Sergey, but peered into the dark as if he was looking for someone. And his mouth was open as if he was about to say something. This above all seemed wrong to Sergey—to look so chatty and wide awake when you were supposed to be dead. But maybe Grandpa Abe was trying to tell Sergey something, to reveal some secret from the Other Side.

Sergey swallowed hard. Whatever Grandpa wanted to tell him, Sergey hoped it wouldn't be scary. He hated scary stuff right at bedtime. Not that scary stuff actually scared him, of course—it just kept him awake at night. But maybe if he gave Grandpa his undivided attention, Grandpa would tell Sergey what he wanted, what he was looking for, why he was hanging around the house.

"Grandpa?" he said softly, in a more trembling voice than he meant to. "How are you? I mean, I know you're dead, but how are things? Is everything okay over there?" Grandpa Abe didn't answer him, just stood there peering around the room, looking as if he were about to speak.

Suddenly, a voice in the darkness rang out. Sergey nearly jumped out of his skin.

"Hopchunurabasticuckoo!" It was Ivan, who had awakened and was staring at him from his sleeping bag.

"You startled me, idiot!" Sergey growled. He reached over and thumped Ivan on the arm. "Why'd you have to do that in the middle of the night?"

"Payback for that time in front of the house, heh-heh-heh," said Ivan. "Besides, I woke up with that word in my head and saw you sitting up. I wondered if you were sitting up in your sleep."

Sergey glanced at the foot of his sleeping bag. Grandpa had faded away. Only a whitish whisp of moonlight remained where he had stood.

~

Ivan," Sergey said urgently, "There's something I need to tell you."

"What?"

"You're not going to believe me."

"Tell me anyway."

"Ivan, you might not believe this, but I've been seeing Grandpa all week. Both in daytime and at night." Sergey let this piece of information sink in before he went on.

Ivan didn't laugh or scoff. Instead his voice dropped to a whisper and he said, "What does he look like?"

"Kind of pale. But still, Ivan, way too lively for a dead person. He eats whole plates of hard-boiled eggs."

"I wondered why I've been craving hard-boiled eggs all week," Ivan said in amazement. "What's he doing here?"

"He's always very busy, Ivan. Looking for stuff. Sitting in his favorite chair."

"Looking for stuff?" Ivan squeaked in a high voice.

"All the time. You know all those junk drawers he always had? He rummages through them," Sergey said. "And in the mornings I've even seen him put on his tefillin and pray the morning prayers."

"He was here tonight, wasn't he?" said Ivan.

"Did you see him too?" Sergey whispered excitedly.

"No. But I've been dreaming about him every night. Tonight I dreamed that he was saying 'hopchunurabasticuckoo'. Then I woke up."

"Why do *I* keep seeing him?" Sergey asked urgently.

"That's a good question," Ivan said frowning. "But it must all mean something."

"Yeah, but what?" Sergey demanded. Ivan was his older brother by three and a half years, and he depended on him for all the major explanations of life—the real ones, after the grown-ups tried to explain things.

"Well, what is it, already?" Sergey said impatiently.

Sergey could hear Ivan tapping on his braces, deep in thought. "Maybe we've been calling him back," Ivan said at last.

"How?" Sergey asked, a shiver running down his spine.

"With all our memories, retelling his jokes, his funny words. Talking about all our happy times together."

"Like saying 'hopchunurabasti—'" began Sergey.

"Sh-sh-sh-sh," said Ivan. "Don't say that word anymore! I think that's part of the problem."

"I don't get it," said Sergey. The rabbi says we're supposed to remember our loved ones. That's sort of how we keep them alive, in our memories," Sergey said.

"I think we're making it hard for him to leave us, Sergey," Ivan said slowly, He's too attached to this house, to Grandma, to us. His spirit can't break away from here."

"So what'll we do?" said Sergey.

Ivan thought for awhile. "I think we have to say *Kaddish.*"

"But we already are. At least you are. And the others are. I don't really. I can't read Hebrew that well yet."

"I remember what Rabbi Meyers taught us in Hebrew school, about saying the *Kaddish,*" Ivan went on, thinking out loud. "How when someone dies, the family is supposed to say *Kaddish* not just during *shivah,* but every day for a whole year. And then once every year, on the anniversary of the person's death. Rabbi Meyers said that it's not just a prayer for the living. It's also a prayer to help the dead person."

"Help him do what?" Sergey asked, wide-eyed.

"Find his way."

"Is he lost?" asked Sergey.

"Yes," Ivan said. "I think he is. He needs the *Kaddish* to help him find the way. Rabbi Meyers says that every time you say the *Kaddish,* it lifts the person's soul up—sort of points them in the right direction, away from the world of the living. Toward heaven. "

Sergey felt another shiver run through him as he thought about what Ivan had said.

"But wait," he said. "If everybody's already saying *Kaddish* three times a day, why does he keep coming back here?"

"Well," Ivan said uncertainly, "maybe because it's just the first week.

Maybe Grandpa needs us—his grandsons—to say *Kaddish,* instead of just remembering all the jokes and good times."

Sergey stared at Ivan, whose face was barely visible in the moonlight, his own eyes wide as saucers. He was glad it was dark and that Ivan couldn't see how scared he felt. "Like I said, I don't read Hebrew so well yet, not like you, Ivan. It's still three years till my Bar Mitzvah," Sergey protested. When it came to praying, Sergey usually mumbled his way shyly through the words. Or else daydreamed in boredom.

"Try, Serge," Ivan said urgently. "Read it in English if you have to, but try to say it out loud and strong."

Both boys grew quiet. Sergey stared out the window as the moonlight receded farther and farther from view. He thought long and hard about what Ivan had said. It made sense. But now he felt the weight of responsibility on his shoulders. He couldn't just coast along behind the grown-ups anymore.

Finally he spoke again, and his voice sounded small and faint in the dark. "I'll do it, Ivan. I'll say *Kaddish.* I'll practice until I'm as good as you," he said to Ivan. He felt grateful to be next to Ivan tonight, to help talk away his fears. "Ivan? Did you hear me?"

But the only reply from the sleeping bag next to him were the soft snoring sounds of his brother, who had fallen back to sleep.

~

Sergey slept fitfully for the rest of the night, but for some reason he didn't feel tired the next morning. When he awoke, Ivan was already dressed and downstairs having breakfast, his sleeping bag neatly rolled up. Sergey jumped up, eager to start the day. He felt relieved that it was the final morning of *shivah.* After the morning service and the final *Kaddish,* they would all be going home, even Grandma. She would be staying with them for several weeks. Sergey thought that was a good idea, just in case Grandpa Abe kept coming back to the house.

At nine o'clock, people crowded into Grandma's house for the final service. The rabbi who had conducted the funeral was there too. He began to speak to the crowd of mourners. *"Kaddish,"* he reminded them, "is known as the traditional prayer for the dead, but strange as it seems, the *Kaddish* doesn't say one word about death or dying. It's a prayer praising God, a declaration of faith in God even in our deepest sorrow. Since ancient times, Jews have believed that the *Kaddish* is healing not only for the loved ones left behind but also for the soul of the deceased."

Everyone rose and began the service. Sergey looked over at Ivan, who was standing across the room near Grandma. All morning Ivan hadn't given the slightest sign that he remembered the talk they'd had last night. For a moment, Sergey wondered if he had dreamed it, dreamed all of it, even Grandpa Abe's appearances. Suddenly the whole week seemed like a dream. And then, across the room, while Sergey was thinking this thought, someone gently slipped in between Ivan and Grandma, and Sergey's heart began to race. It was Grandpa Abe. He had shuffled in again with his prayer book, looking oddly content and at home, as if he intended to hang around indefinitely. He stood there with his prayer book as if he was there to say *Kaddish*——for someone else! Sergey didn't squeeze his eyes shut this time but stared at him, half in dread, half in fascination. He wondered if Grandpa Abe was going to haunt this house, haunt Ivan and him, forever.

"Let us now turn to page fifty-four for the *Kaddish*," said the rabbi.

Pages turned noisily. Grandpa Abe, far from fading away, seemed to be turning his pages too. Neither Ivan nor Grandma seemed to realize he was standing there between them. Grandpa himself didn't seem to notice them either. He seemed to be in his own little world. Sergey was suddenly swept with a wave of true sadness, realizing how much he would miss Grandpa— the real Grandpa, constant and in the flesh.

Across the room, Ivan suddenly looked up as if he sensed something. He turned and stared at Sergey, and Sergey wondered if Ivan felt Grandpa at his side. Ivan tapped the prayer book, looking at Sergey. Sergey understood. He took his eyes away from Ivan and Grandpa Abe to begin reading the *Kaddish.* He wasn't able to read much Hebrew yet. He'd have to read the English transliteration on the other side of the page. He hoped it would count just as much.

Yitgadal, ve-yitkaddash shemei rabba. . . .
Magnified and sanctified be His great Name. . . .

The crowd was large, filling up every corner of the house, and the windows were wide open, letting the morning breeze into the stuffy room. The voices of the mourners saying *Kaddish* echoed loudly off the walls, sending shivers up Sergey's spine. He realized this was the first time he'd ever prayed with all his heart, like a real member of a prayer minyan. He liked the way his own voice blended in with the other voices, making it sound like one single, mighty voice speaking. Sergey kept his eyes glued to the page, concentrating on saying the words.

Oseh shalom bimroma, Hu ya-aseh shalom alenu ve-al kol Yisrael. . . .
Let peace descend on us, on all Israel and all the world. . . .

Suddenly, as the crowd said the final words of *Kaddish,* his eyes began to play tricks on him. Both the English and the Hebrew letters of the *Kaddish* seemed to be floating off the page! He blinked with astonishment and followed the letters upward. But before he could figure out where they were going, Sergey heard a shout of purest joy:

"Hopchunurabasticuckoo!"

Sergey's eyes flew to where his Grandpa had been standing, and he gasped in wonder.

Hundreds of tiny black wings were flapping before his eyes, sweeping fast across the room. The letters of the *Kaddish* had turned into mighty wings, lifting a joyful Grandpa Abe through the open window, carrying him upward toward heaven.

~ Background Note from the Author ~

Hopchunurabasticuckoo is the word my Grandpa Spector made up to delight the grandchildren in our large family. He had grown up speaking Yiddish and Russian in a tiny Jewish village in Russia. When he escaped to America, he never became fluent in English as my grandmother did. Rather, he spoke "Yenglish"—part Yiddish, part English, with a little Russian thrown in—as many Jewish immigrants did, making new, often hilarious words from a mixture of all three languages.

Another thing about Grandpa was that he saved everything. He had grown up a poor boy in his Russian-Jewish village. In America, in his tiny Kansas City bungalow, he kept everything. From buttons to furniture, to knickknacks and coins and all kinds of papers, he never threw anything away. Like Grandpa Abe in my story, he was forever rummaging around in his drawers, retrieving things or finding space for new things. I picture him still rummaging in his heavenly closets and drawers.

~ About the Author ~

DEBORAH SPECTOR SIEGEL is the author of the acclaimed young adult novel about the Spanish Inquisition, *The Cross by Day, The Mezuzzah by Night,* published by The Jewish Publication Society in 1999. She has also written articles and feature stories for Jewish and secular publications in Chicago and the Midwest for more than twenty years, including the *Chicago Tribune.* She lives in Buffalo Grove, Illinois, with her husband and two teenage sons.

L'Dor V'Dor
(From Generation to Generation)

~ Lois Ruby ~

Grandpa Mel's bow tie hangs open as he scans the sports page. Ezra tries to read box scores from the back side, but the words jump around. His chest itches. Maybe dark, curly hairs are starting to grow. More likely it's the scratchy letters of the T-shirt that he's turned inside out. Grandpa doesn't appreciate the name of the band: the Anti-Femites. Jeeze, it's not like some anti-Semitic message. Girls, *women,* might be insulted, but not Jews. Grandpa's hypersensitive because he was one of the soldiers of the Seventh Army who'd liberated a Nazi death camp in Germany.

Grandpa had described the scene to him once, just after Dad left. (It was so much easier to think of Dad as *gone* instead of dead.) Grandpa had said, "A picture like that, Ezra, it burns an image in your mind until you take your last breath." It had all happened so many years ago. What difference could it make *now*? Ezra had tried with all his energy not to hear Grandpa's words, but they scorched his unwilling memory anyway.

"It was April 29, 1945. We found thirty-two thousand people with arms and legs like twigs. Folds of skin flapping against brittle bone. You could hardly tell the men from the women. Eyes like ghosts, sunken, milky. They were too weak to show surprise when we arrived. The other guys and me, we cried plenty; believe me, Ezra, we cried the tears those poor souls were too tired to shed. It was tough on all of us, but for us Jewish soldiers, well . . ." His voice faded away. "We couldn't do enough fast enough—feed the starving, treat the sick, bury the dead who were stacked like cords of wood."

Ezra couldn't help registering the pain of fifty-five years ago still fresh in Grandpa's eyes. And in some ways, it had helped him put the thing about Dad out of his mind.

"Black and white stripes, that's what they wore. To this day I can't even wear a striped tie," Grandpa had told him.

So, Ezra turns his Anti-Femites shirt inside out.

Something flutters behind him. Probably Mom shaking the folds of a billowy scarf, in her usual frenzy to get ready for work. Ezra turns around. No one's there. And now the pipes down the hall groan as Mom's shower goes on.

This isn't the first time since Grandpa's visit that Ezra *knows* someone is standing behind him, only to find nothing but shimmery air, like on an afternoon at Lake Merrill.

Grandpa begins working his bow tie into a complicated clownlike knot, using the toaster as a mirror. "Fit for a fight?" he asks himself. "I sure will be glad when this trial's over so I can go home."

"You're not leaving before my Bar Mitzvah, are you, Grandpa?"

"That's a month off, kiddo. I'd drive your mother nuts hanging around here that long. Besides, I've got to work a trial in Detroit next week." He tosses Ezra the sports page. "Living out of a suitcase is no fun, but that's the life of an itinerant forensics specialist, right, my boy?"

In a minute Grandpa's out the door, and Ezra ponders what to do with this cloudy gift of a summer day. Then he's *sure* someone is in the room! He spins around and spots a boy about his age. "Hey, how did you get in here?"

The boy seems to fold into himself like a Chinese fan, ever thinner. Not like a fan; like a card sliding between two other cards in the deck until it disappears. Ezra blinks. The *whole deck* has vanished!

"Where did you go?" Ezra demands, feeling like an idiot talking to an empty room.

Here. The voice is thin; the "r" trilled.

"Listen, you can't scare me." Ezra's knees knock under the table, while his eyes jump to every shadow of the room. To prove his bravery, he pops a spoonful of soggy Cheerios in his mouth.

Down the hall, the water goes off and the shower door clatters.

The fan, the giant deck of cards, unfolds again, and a full-size boy stands on the other side of the table. Too weird!

The boy's hair is nearly yellow and parted down the middle. Some of it sticks out like wheat over a scarecrow's ear. Eyes the color of faded blue jeans search Ezra's face. The clothes are way out of style—a plaid flannel shirt buttoned to the throat and overalls of some material that looks like the stuff they make canteens out of, canvas, yeah, and brown, leather, old-man shoes.

"Where'd you come from? And you'd better talk fast before my father gets in here." As if Dad could actually show up.

From over there. The boy points vaguely over his shoulder.

"Where?" Ezra snaps.

English not good. Cherman.

"Oh, I get it. You're from Germany. You're staying next door with the Ralstons. They always have exchange students. Don't worry. In another week you'll be wearing Nikes and Old Navy stuff."

Then a curious thing happens. The boy begins talking in German, and Ezra understands every word as his brain instantly translates a language he's never heard.

"Helmut? They actually name guys that in your country? Bair-leen? Oh, you mean Berlin, yeah, I've heard of it. Munich, yeah, I've heard of that, too."

Helmut is pelting Ezra with bits of information until Ezra sucks in his breath at one word: "Dachau?" he says quietly.

Dachau is the camp Grandpa liberated.

"Ezra!" Mom yells. "Do you see my car keys anywhere?"

Helmut begins folding again, fading.

"Wait! Don't go!" Ezra grabs the keys and rattles them for Mom's ears, as Helmut vanishes into the shimmering air.

He'd better tell Mom. But can't! She'll think he's feverish, and she'll want to stay home from work, and without Dad, every penny counts. Okay, then he'll tell Davey Krug.

What, and look like he's totally crazy?

"Helmut?" he whispers. But there's no response—not a ripple of air, not even the cuckoo clock, the only witness, singing proof that seconds ago a blond, blue-eyed stranger had stood in this room talking about Dachau.

~

Two threads of a dream battle for prime time in Ezra's night. The Falcons have won the middle school tournament, and Ezra's the starting pitcher at State.

Right. He didn't even make the team. But it's a dream.

Championship game, bottom of the ninth. Falcons lead by a run, and everything hinges on his pitch.

Ezra's stare spooks the batter, who's got two strikes on him already. The stands are silent, the cheerleaders frozen in place, and the only sound on the field is the taunt of his teammates. "Here . . . batter-batter-batter-batter. . . ."

As he rocks back to fire the pitch, the chatter bleeds into another chant: "The sins of the fathers, third and fourth, the sins of the fathers, third and fourth." He turns to see what's happened to his infield, and every base is manned by Helmut in canvas overalls, and every baseman is rumbling the chant: "The sins of the fathers are visited upon the children, and the children's children, to the third and fourth generation." *What?*

Ezra is jarred out of the dream by something pinging against his window. He darts up. Clock says three-eighteen in blaring red. And then a head darkens the window shade.

He wants to yell, "Grandpa!" but his throat is paralyzed. He slides out of bed, *under* the bed, clutching the sheet.

"Ezra," he hears faintly. "It's me. Open the window, little brother."

Heart pounding with relief, Ezra scurries across the room, snaps up the shade, cranks the window, and there's Josh grinning.

"Wanna go for a moonlight canoe ride?"

~

Paddling out on Lake Merrill, Josh says, "What good is a brother in college if he can't sneak home and rescue you once in a while?"

Josh basically ignored Ezra for the first twelve years of Ezra's life, then surfaced suddenly right after Dad's car wreck.

Ezra trails his hands through the bathwater-warm lake. He sees blue eyes everywhere, Helmut's eyes—in the trees on the bank, in a dog streaming by along the shore, in the moon.

"Josh? Don't take this wrong, okay?" His brother's face shines in the moonlight, open and ready. "Do we believe in ghosts?"

"We Millers? We Jews? We mortals? What?"

"We—you and me."

Josh lays the paddle across the canoe, and they drift lazily through the still, black water. "What's going on?"

A tulle fog rises from the lake, and Ezra watches it take the form of a dim, wavering boy. Helmut; but Josh sees none of this.

"You know Dachau?"

"Yeah?" Josh says warily.

"And how Grandpa and the other guys liberated the camp after the war?"

Josh nods.

"Well, somebody from there has been visiting me."

"A survivor?"

"A kid my age."

"I don't get it, Ez."

"A ghost. I don't think he's a survivor. I think he was a guard at Dachau."

Josh sighs and begins paddling back to shore.

Sharp, guttural words pierce the gentle wind. "Hear that, Josh? It's German."

"I don't hear anything."

"Wait." Ezra cocks his head to listen. "He's the son of an SS guard at Dachau. He's telling me about it." Ezra translates as fast as the wind delivers the words:

Every night my father came home to us. He washed away the stench. We ate, we laughed. Sundays we went to the park, Mama, Papa, Gerte, and me. A loud, brassy band played in the park. We marched to the music. Hup-hup-hup!

"Ezra! Snap out of it," Josh whispers, but Ezra is still listening, trancelike. Why is Helmut haunting him? What does he want? The ghostly voice floats in Ezra's mind again:

My birthday, April 29, 1945, my twelfth, but there were only two candles, and the cake was really just a small tart because it was wartime; there were shortages. And my father did not come home that night.

"Ezra?" Josh waves his hand in front of Ezra's face.

And your father?

"Gone," Ezra replies. Then he owns up to the truth. "Dead."

My father, dead also. Mine was a good father, but an evil man. Yours was a good man, but he did an evil thing leaving you so early.

"Yes!"

"You're scaring me, Ez. We're going home and waking Mom and

Grandpa." Josh begins paddling frantically.

"Not yet." The words come from Ezra's mouth, but in Helmut's voice.

~

The next day, Helmut says, *We are two of a kind.*

They can talk now without actual words clogging the air between them.

Ezra is pedaling his bike to Davey Krug's, and Helmut hovers over the handlebars, solid as ice, except that he melts as soon as Ezra reaches for him. He leaves no puddle, not even so much as freeze-dried granules.

Now he's behind Ezra.

Two of a kind, you and I.

Ezra speeds up. A breeze dries the sweat on his tank top. Hottest day of the year, KROC Radio said, and still Helmut has his flannel shirt buttoned to his ears. His breath, seeping like air from a basketball, beads the sweat on Ezra's neck and sends a chill down his back.

Ezra is determined to ignore Helmut as he pumps his way toward Davey's. But curiosity wins out.

"How are we alike?" Ezra asks.

I thought you would never ask! Ach, we have both inherited something from Dachau. The guilt of German fathers is my inheritance. Yours is the grief of Jewish fathers. See?

"I don't see!"

It is all about balance. You see how you balance on this bicycle? What will happen if you throw your weight to the right?

Suddenly the bike pulls away from Ezra and caroms into a shallow ditch, Ezra on top of it. Furious, he yanks the bike to its wheels and leads it back up to the road.

"Leave me alone!"

I have come to you because you and I are out of balance. My guilt is stronger than your grief.

"What grief? I didn't even know anybody at Dachau."

That is my very point. You haven't even discovered your grief yet, but I'm drowning in my own guilt.

"You're the one who's giving me grief." Ezra pedals harder and streaks past trees and houses, but the road ahead is longer than ever.

Jewish children are born with the sorrow, friend, and German children are born with the guilt. We cannot stop it.

"Get away from me," Ezra shouts, and he breaks free, finally able to close the gap between *here* and *there,* to Davey's house.

~

Grandpa Mel, the DNA expert, is also a pro at shelling roasted peanuts. He can crack one with his teeth, extract the nut with his tongue, and spit the shell into a coffee can in two seconds.

Ezra is much clumsier. There's a mess of shells and peanut dust around his feet, while Grandpa is rapidly filling the can like an efficient machine.

It's dark on the back porch because a giant pine tree hides the sliver of moon. Helmut is quiet, but Ezra knows he's there, waiting, always waiting.

"Grandpa, do you believe in ghosts?"

"Well," he says—crack, crunch, *phoot* into the can—"I have to in my line of work. Dead bodies have stories to tell me."

"Must be creepy."

Ezra senses Helmut shifting uneasily. Maybe Helmut doesn't want his own story told. Or maybe he's afraid it'll be told wrong, and that the balance he's always wailing about will get totally out of whack, like a seesaw with a second-grader on one end and a grizzly on the other.

"No, it's not at all creepy. I figure these bodies hold secrets they're dying to reveal. Their spirits can't rest until somebody unlocks the past for them. That's my job. I'm in the business of laying ghosts to rest. Not real ghosts, you understand. I'm talking about the unanswered questions that haunt survivors. My job is to set things right again."

You see, Ezra? It is all about balance.

"You mean, putting things in balance, Grandpa?"

"You could say that."

The moon gliding across the sky peeks out from behind the giant pine to reveal a squirrel trying to claim his share from the bowl of peanuts.

Helmut discharges nervous energy like Fourth of July sparklers.

I do not like animals. They have an uncanny sixth sense.

"Wow, a double," Grandpa says, mumbling around the load in his mouth. "Both of 'em sweet and crisp as an apple."

The squirrel skitters away, and Ezra feels Helmut relax. Then Grandpa surprises him:

"Seeing ghosts, Ezra?"

"No, no, I just—"

Tell him.

Grandpa says, "We're coming up on the first anniversary of your father's death, kiddo. Maybe there's some unfinished business, something you need from him, or something he wants to transmit to you before your Bar Mitzvah. Could be you're unconsciously calling him back to clear up the static on that radio message."

Ezra stands up, turns his back to Grandpa. "No, it's not Dad."

"Who, then?"

You can tell him. Ezra feels Helmut pushing him forward, as surely as if his hands were on Ezra's narrow shoulders. He's thrown off balance and kicks over the coffee can. Shells scatter to the night. The wind herds them back into a tight pile, like autumn leaves.

We Germans like order

"You'll think I'm crazy, Grandpa."

"Kiddo, my philosophy is we've all got to be a little crazy, or it's not worth the trip."

"Maybe I haven't figured out how to mourn for dead people. I mean, they don't teach it in school or Boy Scouts or Bar Mitzvah class."

Grandpa scrapes his chair over toward Ezra, not touching, but so close that barely a breeze can pass between them. Helmut is pushed out of the space, but lurks there, expectantly.

"When your father died, Ezra, you thought you had to hold in all that sorrow or anger, or whatever it was you were feeling. We all cried, even your brother, but your eyes were dry all through those days of *shivah*."

He remembers feeling empty, like these peanut shells, crust and dust with nothing inside.

"Your mother worried so much about you, but I said, 'Judith, give the boy space. He'll cry in his own way, in his own time.'"

"Grandpa?"

"Yes, son?"

"Am I responsible for anything bad my father did?"

"Your dad was a kind man, kiddo. I never knew him to do anything bad."

"No, no," Ezra says impatiently. "I mean, am I . . . are you . . . responsible for the bad things people did before we were even born?"

Yes, that is the question! Helmut urges him on. *Am I guilty of my father's sins?*

"That's what the Bible says, over and over, Ezra, but, to tell you the truth, I don't believe it. Judaism believes that we're each born brand-new with clean slates, and we can fill those slates with good deeds or with not-so-good deeds. Our job is to draw the pictures on our slates with our own screechy chalk, you get it?" He shoots a peanut shell across Ezra's lap into the pyramid.

"Grandpa, do you hate Germans? I mean like the children of the children who were guards at Dachau?"

Grandpa Mel, always so quick with an answer, now draws into himself and sighs.

You see? You see? Helmut taunts.

"No, son, I do not hate Germans, but neither can I forget what happened two, three generations ago."

A long silence hangs between them like a sailor's rope, thick enough to save them from drowning.

Helmut offers him a frayed end of the rope. It feels so real in his hand. *Pull one end, and I will pull the other. A tug-of-war.*

Is that the way? Ezra just doesn't know.

See the line in the dirt?

Ezra sees it now, a straight, one-inch gully between him and Helmut. They each toe the line. He asks, "What if we tug and pull and it's a standoff? I don't give an inch, and you don't give a centimeter. Will we be pulling forever?"

No, no! We will win in the balance.

Something doesn't compute here. "You know, I'm a lot stronger than you," Ezra says. "I'm flesh-and-blood, but you're only a ghost. I could easily pull you over to my side." There's the slightest hesitation, enough to make Ezra suspicious. The rope is nearly alive, thrumming with possibilities. Ezra gives it a tentative tug in his mind, but Helmut jerks his end, throwing Ezra totally off-kilter. Is it a power play—or a dare?

Grandpa notices nothing and goes on shelling peanuts and tossing shells. Ezra longs to shout, "What should I do, Grandpa!" but something tells him he must finish this tug-of-war on his own.

Helmut cries, *Pull! Balanced, we can make the past vanish like dust. It is our only chance.*

Ezra hears Helmut's promise and also feels the warmth of Grandpa's arm that makes the hair on his own neck stand up. Grandpa can't forget Dachau. Who could? The past can *never* vanish like dust. This idea floods Ezra with a deep sadness. And then he suddenly understands why Helmut is so eager for this tug-of-war. He wants Ezra to pull him to his side of the gully, to the good side. It's the only way Helmut will ever be free of the guilt he feels for his father's brutalities. But if Helmut is stronger, or if he's as evil as his father was, and if Ezra is weak and unsure of himself, Helmut will pull Ezra over to *his* side. Ezra will never be free again. He's got to escape!

Now he's absolutely sure of one thing: escape is with Grandpa, the liberator. Ezra has to hike his way through his own unplowed sadness as well as Grandpa Mel's stored-up sorrow. He's sure of it now: if they make the journey back together, they'll all three be freed. Gone will be the ghosts of the cruel guards, the survivors, and even Dad will be able to rest in peace.

"What your father did, it's not your fault, Helmut, any more than it's my father's fault, or my fault that my father died." Helmut frantically tries to lure Ezra with the rope again, but Ezra is clear about what he must do.

"You've just got to trust me, Helmut."

Desperate now, Helmut rears back and pulls the rope with all his might, but Ezra drops his end. Helmut staggers back, back, back, until he vanishes into the black night, and Ezra can breathe freely once again.

Catching a peanut shell in midflight, he says, "Grandpa, talk to me. I think it's time you told me about Dachau."

His grandfather raises his eyebrows in surprise, then puts a firm arm around Ezra's shoulders. "A glorious spring day, April 29, 1945," he begins. "We have just burst through the barbed-wire gates. . . ."

~ Background Note from the Author ~

Ghosts that appear as ethereal, spooky specters do not interest me. The ghosts that haunt the human heart and our collective history do. I see the ghosts of the Holocaust shimmering on two fronts: in the descendants of survivors and witnesses, and in the descendants of perpetrators. I wondered how this haunting fits with the Torah concept: "...I, the LORD your God am an impassioned God, visiting the guilt of the parents upon the children, upon the third and upon the fourth generations of those who reject Me. . ." (Exod. 20:5). And I wondered, What does this say to a child? Is this fair? Is this Jewish?

And then I asked myself, What would happen if descendants of both hauntings encountered one another? Would they cancel each other out? Would they bring flesh and bone to one another? Or would their meeting finally allow both ghosts to rest in peace? Yes, I decided, it would bring peace.

~ About the Author ~

LOIS RUBY says that she wallows in books. Some three thousand surround her in her home office, and ten of them are books she wrote herself. She has worked for the Dallas Public Library and the University of Missouri Library and has been the librarian of her synagogue for nearly three decades. She has also been a waitress, a statistical typist, a day camp director, a youth group advisor, and director of the Wichita (Kansas) Jewish Community School. She says that she much prefers writing, and visiting schools where she talks about writing, to all those other jobs.

She has been married to Thomas Ruby, a clinical psychologist, for thirty-five years and they have three grown sons. She is on the boards of Inter-Faith Inn, a homeless shelter, and the Wichita Public Library. Outside of her family, she says, the place she feels most comfortable is among teenagers, laughing.

The Ghost Well

~ Ann Manheimer ~

The first time it happened we were in this grand and spooky old mansion, the kind of place where you expect things to happen.

Adam, my twin brother, and I were going to have our party there, after our B'nai Mitzvah. We were doing the whole thing together—the ceremony and the celebration—because Mom couldn't afford two and didn't want to ask Dad for help, what with his not being Jewish and living so far away. It wasn't the way I wanted it, but what did that matter?

Like the Bat Mitzvah itself. I mean, I knew why Mom wanted me to do it; she'd told me enough about when she was active in the women's movement. And Bubbe wanted me to because of her family being killed by Nazis. And Adam's wanting it had something to do with Adam taking Dad's place at the head of a community, and also with his being brilliant and doing everything right and everybody telling him so all the time.

Me? I didn't have a clue. It was just assumed I'd have—I mean, become, that's what you're supposed to say—a Bat Mitzvah. So when the time came along, I went along. And when Mom said Adam and I had to have ours together, I went along then, too. Like always.

So there we were in the mansion, sampling the food and choosing napkins for our party, and I didn't even have a word of my *derash* written yet. That's the thing you have to write explaining the Torah portion you have to read. You're supposed to show how smart you are and everything. Well, writing's just about the only thing I'm okay at, but I couldn't even do that for my Bat Mitzvah.

At least, I thought, I could help choose the napkins. A lady brought us a pile of them and said we should select two colors. Mom told us to each choose one, but they should go together. Adam picked sea foam—it was the only color not named for a food. I thought salmon sort of went with that, both ideawise and colorwise, so I chose that.

"*Pink?*" Adam's mouthful of squished ravioli hung open.

"Allie gets her choice too, Adam," Mom said in her teacher voice.

"But *Mo-om!* You can't have *pink* for a Bar Mitzvah!"

"It isn't pink," the lady started, "it's . . ."

I shrugged. What did it matter? Adam would get his way in the end.

"He does have a point, Allie," Mom said.

So I started to reach for another color, not caring which, and that's when it began. First, everybody stopped moving and talking, like they'd frozen in place, Adam still showing his mushed-up ravioli. Second, I got all cold, with chills and goose bumps and everything. Then a wind started blowing around the room and I heard something echoing, like somebody calling out in a valley or down a well, making their voice hollow and spooky, saying something like, "*Listen . . . listen. . . .*"

Listen to what? I wondered. Napkins?

Then it passed, so fast I thought maybe nothing had happened.

But something had. My hand, which had been on its way to picking up a blueberry-colored napkin, just stopped in midair.

"Allie? Did you want to choose something else?" Mom asked.

"Uh," I answered brilliantly.

The lady flashed a big lipstick smile. "Perhaps you'd like to think about it some more."

We left right after that, but I couldn't stop thinking about what happened. Had I really heard something? What was I supposed to listen to? And who was telling me to?

For some reason —maybe because it was getting close to Purim—I'd been thinking about Queen Vashti, the queen before Esther who got in trouble for refusing King Ahasuerus's order to "show her beauty," whatever that means. How could she refuse when everyone expected her to do what he said? Maybe she heard a weird voice, too.

Nobody knows what ever happened to her; it didn't get written down. That always made me sad. I wrote a story about her once, that she started a colony for women who wouldn't listen to their husbands, and they told each other stories and danced together every night. I never showed it to anybody, though. I never showed anyone stuff I wrote.

But then I thought, am I going nuts? Maybe I was getting something, like a brain tumor. Maybe I ought to tell somebody. I didn't want to worry

Mom or Bubbe, Dad would just talk about my active imagination, and my best friend was out of town.

That left Adam. Not too bad a choice, actually. I mean, he really *is* smart.

"You really *are* crazy."

Great.

"Just because we were in an old building, you start hearing voices? Who do you think it was—the ghost of Bat Mitzvahs past?"

For a second I thought maybe it was. But there aren't many Bat Mitzvahs past. None in my family.

Then Adam's tone changed. I think he was trying to help, though it can be hard to tell. "Look, nobody else heard that voice. It had to be just your imagination."

He paused as if he wanted to say more. Then he did.

"I know you don't care a whole lot about this Bat Mitzvah, but just deal with it. It'll make Mom and Bubbe happy. It doesn't have to be that big a thing—I mean, you don't need to start making up ghostly voices when you ought to be writing your speech, which—do I need to remind you?—is two weeks late."

I knew that.

Adam had turned his in two weeks early, of course. He got the best part of our portion, about the red heifer. The rabbi explained that it's all about life and death.

My portion was about the Hebrews being thirsty in the desert. Big surprise. How much can you say about that? If I wasn't becoming a Bat Mitzvah, I wouldn't have to figure it out.

That thought stopped me. I pushed the door to my room behind me and stared at my *humash,* the book you use to practice reading your Torah portion. It was open on my bed, along with a blank pad where I was supposed to be writing my *derash.*

What if I really didn't go through with it? Maybe that's what the voice meant—that if I didn't want to go through with my Bat Mitzvah, I should refuse to, like Vashti. Mom wouldn't have wasted anything, she'd still have Adam's stuff, the party would go on. It would just happen without me making a fool of myself.

I mean, isn't that what it's all about? Everybody watching to see if you do better or worse than the last kid or than they did themselves? If you're brilliant like Adam, you get lots of congratulations. If you're a mess-up like me, everybody forces a smile and you feel worse than ever.

I didn't want to make Mom and Bubbe unhappy. But the idea of saying no to something everybody else wanted me to do made me feel like something inside was waking up.

~

I plopped down on my rug, picked up the pad to write but started doodling instead, and that's when it happened again. No wind this time. This time, it was more like fire—my room got all hot and close, I got real sweaty, my pencil sort of took over and started drawing flames and buildings with black smoke belching out and barbed wire, and then that echo-ey voice came back: *"Listen . . . listen. . . ."*

I threw the pencil down as if *it* were on fire.

Then I saw Bubbe's feet in my doorway. I guess I hadn't shut the door completely, because she knocks when it's closed. She comes over a lot, especially since my folks split up.

"This pencil offends you, Allie?"

She says stuff in a way that makes you laugh and think at the same time.

"Oh, hi, Bubbe. I was just . . ."

"What is this?" She picked up the pad and stared hard at the pictures. "What were you drawing? It is . . ." Her eyes got misty, her head was shaking. "Why did you make this?"

"I didn't mean to. I don't even know what it is."

That wasn't true. I didn't want to know. I'd heard about the concentration camps and how Bubbe survived and went to Israel and fought for independence.

She sat slowly on my bed. I looked at her comfortable shoes, her beige pants, her close-cropped white hair. She stared at the picture and shook her head for a long time.

"How could you know this?" she said finally. "It is amazing. This is not such knowledge as I would wish for you. But it is good that you have it."

Her eyes wandered around my room—the shelves crammed with books, the porcelain dolls crowded under the Rebeltones poster, my desk stuffed with half-written poems and stories.

She sighed. "What we would have given to have what you have."

My stomach twisted. I tried not to say anything—I mean, this is my grandma, I love her—but I was so tired of that stuff. It seems like everywhere you look, that's what you hear—Jews suffered, so be grateful and feel guilty.

Words came out without my meaning them to. "I'm sorry it was hard for you, Bubbe." They got faster. "But does that mean I can't live my own life? I just want to be normal—talk to my friends, do homework, watch TV. I don't want to feel bad about having nice stuff. And I don't want to feel bad about feeling bad about my little problems just 'cause they're not big like yours were."

"That's not what I mean." She spoke really gently.

I was shaking.

"I mean this Bat Mitzvah," she said. "It troubles you."

How did she know?

"I do not know why it does. It is very important, what you do. You must understand, we were victims. We did not have such an opportunity. So many thirsted for it—my own sister wanted to be a rabbi, but it was not heard of for women in those days. And then came the Nazis . . . but even before them—in the Inquisition and other times—so many died, men and women, who will always be nameless. It is for them, Allie. Remember the ones who went before. Do not let the Nazis win by refusing your place among our people."

For some reason, all I could think of after she left was that thing Adam said about the ghost of Bat Mitzvahs past. It was like Bubbe was saying I had to become a Bat Mitzvah for all those Bat Mitzvahs that never happened.

That sort of made sense.

But it wasn't enough.

~

The third time was the weirdest. No wind or fire—this time, it was an earthquake.

I was in the rabbi's office. He was disappointed I hadn't started my derash. "Perhaps you need more help, Al—"

His eyes went all buggy when it hit. It wasn't big. In California, you get used to little earthquakes. But he'd just moved from the East and got so scared that he froze.

Then I heard that voice again, echoing like in a well, "Listen . . . listen . . . ."

So I listened. Stuff was rattling. It sounded like tambourines playing.

It *was* tambourines playing. Well, *a* tambourine.

What made it so weird was that suddenly a beautiful, old woman was there, tapping the tambourine, her silver hair wrapped in a braid, her white dress draped from one shoulder.I got chills and sweats at the same time, and my mouth dropped open like a puppet's. I was glad I wasn't eating ravioli.

"Allie."

That echo-ey voice.

"Uh . . . Miriam?" I gasped. I was thinking of Moses' sister because she dies in the Torah chapter right before my part.

She smiled and nodded.

"Is it you I've been hearing?"

She smiled again, closed-mouth. If not for the thousands of years between, I'd've thought she was Mona Lisa.

She wasn't saying anything, so I said, "I don't understand. What do you want me to listen to? Or who? Why are you here anyway?"

There was an instant of silence, then she said, "I am here to give you what you need."

What I needed was somebody to write my *derash.* I didn't think she meant that.

"I bring you . . ." she paused dramatically, *"be'er."*

She pointed to a low, circular stone wall I hadn't noticed, near the rabbi's desk. It looked like a well.

"You brought me a well of *beer*?" I squeaked.

She Mona Lisa'd again. "*Be'er* means well in Hebrew. I bring you the well God gave to our people."

She was talking about my Torah portion. Weird as it sounds, when they were thirsty in the desert, God gave the ancient Hebrews a well they carried around with them. The rabbi said it was a metaphor for the Torah.

"Thanks, but I'm not thirsty."

"There are many kinds of thirst," she said. "The Torah does not mention this, but the stories say God gave the well in my honor."

"Huh?"

"How can I explain? My brother heard God in a burning bush, but most of us do not see such things. Most of us are more like Elijah, my fellow prophet, who listened in wind, earthquake, and fire, and heard God only afterward, in a still, small voice. For me, it is in the quiet depths."

"You're giving me a *well?* But I'm not an ancient Hebrew. I can't carry it."

"I give you the story."

"What about all that stuff about listening? What about my *derash?* What about the napkins?"

We still hadn't chosen our napkins.

She put her finger to her lips, motioned to the well, and then faded away. But the well stayed, even after the rabbi unfroze and acted as if nothing had happened except an earthquake. I didn't think he could see the well.

But I could.

And I kept on seeing it, in different places, like English class and the cantor's office and my room. Nobody else saw it, so I didn't say anything. Mom would send me to a shrink if she found out. If my mom had been Moses' mom, she'd've sent *him* to a shrink.

I didn't touch it or anything. It gave me the creeps—like somebody who wants to be your friend and keeps saying hi, and you're not sure if you want to be friends so you just ignore them.

~

I was still all confused about my Bat Mitzvah. I'd think about Vashti and feel like I should refuse. I'd think about Bubbe and feel like I should do it. But with everybody expecting me to, it's not as if I had a choice. Except whether to like it or not.

I scribbled a speech to turn in to the rabbi, thanking everybody for all the work I'd done and sticking in stuff he'd said about the well being a metaphor for the Torah. You can bet that well stuck at my side while I was writing, no matter where I moved to get away from it.

I went along with Adam about the napkins. Why not? Blueberry made him happy, something I wouldn't be even with pink. I mean salmon.

So that's the way it was. I'd go through with it, but I wouldn't like it. Then they'd be glad and I'd be done.

~

It was the night before. Adam and I were each in our rooms. He was practicing his speech. I was staring at mine. I hated it; all it had were the rabbi's ideas, not mine. I didn't want to say it, just like I didn't want to do the whole thing. It was going to be the worst day of my life, and there was nothing I could do about it.

That's when the well glimmered into view again, right in front of my desk. It was more interesting than my crummy *derash,* so I stared at it. I guess it was pretty, for a well, with different-size rocks, and kind of silver-shimmery. Suddenly, I really wanted to know what it felt like and looked like inside. I mean, how many chances do you get to look down a ghost well?

I moved right next to it. The stones felt cold and bumpy but barely there, like touching rain. I leaned over to look down. The air was damp and sweet, like a cave or a waterfall, and it was so dark you couldn't see the bottom or the sides, only a tiny patch of light on the surface that reflected my desk, with half its drawers sticking out because they were stuffed too full.

Then everything got really quiet. I couldn't hear Adam practicing or Mom clattering the dishes. It was as if the only things that existed were me and the well. And the only echo I could hear came from my own breath.

And that's when I knew.

It wasn't somebody else's voice I was supposed to listen to. Or not listen to. It was my own.

Because when you listen to your own voice, when you make your own choices, you're writing your own story.

And that's what it was all about. Becoming a Bat Mitzvah because it's part of the story.

My part of the story.

Maybe I wouldn't do as good a job as Adam. My brother's a pretty tough act to follow—but then, so was Miriam's brother, and that didn't stop her.

It was okay that I gave in to him about the napkins. Blueberry was fine, and it didn't mean that much to me.

But my *derash* did. I didn't really think the well stood only for the Torah, like the rabbi said. I thought it also stood for what's inside me, inside everyone. For the stuff we make our choices with.

When I thought that, the well kind of grew warmer, shimmered a little more, then faded away. Somehow I knew it wouldn't come back, and that made me kind of sad, but it was okay. I didn't need it anymore.

What I needed was to write.

I picked up my pencil and started a new *derash*. The real one. The one I really would say tomorrow, at my Bat Mitzvah, at the beginning of my story.

~ Background Note from the Author ~

The day of my older daughter's Bat Mitzvah, I stood on the *bimah* and realized for the first time how crowded a synagogue truly is— with people who are there, of course, but also with those we wish were there, and with those we never knew who have gone before us. In this story I decided to search for someone who could stand for all those spirits we encounter at B'nai Mitzvah. I've always thought of the prophet Miriam as one of the true (if unsung) heroes of our past. And when I found the story of her well, I knew that she was the ghost—and the well was the vessel—that could carry the weight of history we encounter whenever a teenager steps forward to take his or her place in our heritage.

~ About the Author ~

ANN MANHEIMER spent her childhood in Los Angeles reading, daydreaming, and playing "Little Women" in "houses" that she and the other neighborhood girls made out of sheets hung on clotheslines in the backyards of their apartment buildings. She has done stints in camp counseling, child care, radio news reporting, newspaper and magazine writing, and practicing law. Now she substitute-teaches in elementary and middle schools and writes stories. Her work has appeared in *Bruce Coville's Book of Nightmares II: More Tales to Make You Scream* and in *Cricket* and *Cicada* magazines. She lives in a house overlooking the San Francisco Bay, with two daughters, her spouse, two black cats, and no known ghosts.

Forgive Me

~ Jerry Raik ~

I t was the middle of September. Summer was over, school had started, and the holidays were coming. The sun was bright; the air, crisp and clean. We knew there wouldn't be many more of those great days before the next spring. Soon after the holidays the clocks would change, and after school it would be cold and dark.

By the time we got to the park, we were already running, and running fast. There were four of us, like always. Me and Jess—Jessica, my best friend—and Sari and Gabe. The park was the same one we always went to, although it wasn't really a park. It wasn't even a playground. It was bounded by the El—elevated train tracks—on one side, the Grand Central Parkway on another, and some particularly ugly factory buildings on the other two sides. There were no trees, grass, monkey bars, or sandboxes. Just concrete surrounded by a cyclone fence, with some benches along the edges. It was really quite an ugly place, but we liked it because it was all ours.

Hardly anyone ever went there—just us and one old lady. One old lady who always got there after we did, sat on the same bench at the far end, and left after we were gone. She was tiny and ancient and ragged. She always wore the same gray wool coat, frayed around the bottom and at the cuffs, and the same black kerchief around her head so you couldn't see her hair. She wore black leather shoes with laces and heavy high heels, and she always carried the same two shiny shopping bags, one black and one red. She never said anything, and she never did anything but watch, but as the days and weeks passed, she got pretty scary to us, just sitting there like that.

"She's crazy," Gabe said one time.

"How do you know?" I asked.

"She is," Jessica said. "She's one of those . . . I can't remember what my dad called them . . . but they're all crazy."

"Or worse." Nobody even asked what Sari meant by that.

We never made a rule about it or even said anything about it, but little by little, we began to leave her alone at her end of the park. We didn't throw or run in her direction or go anywhere near her, if we could help it. If a ball happened to get away and roll down near where she sat, the kid who touched it last would slowly walk down to get it while the rest of us stopped what we were doing and watched. The kid, always looking at the woman except for a few quick glances back to make sure everyone was still there, would snatch up the ball and run back like a mouse being chased by a cat. When the ball and kid were both back and safe, everyone always laughed and giggled and began playing again. We were sure we had just made it— had just survived something terrible that the "crazy old witch" was about to do to us.

~

On that September day, though, I guess because of the great weather, we forgot all that, forgot the old woman completely. We were running faster and faster and throwing farther and farther all the time. We were playing "Salugi" that day. Keep away. Everyone throws the ball or whatever it is you're playing with and tries to keep it away from the one kid who is It. Sari was It. Gabe threw the ball to Jess, and Sari just missed him. Jess ran away a bit and threw to me, and I threw it to Gabe. Then Gabe to Jess, and Jess back to Gabe. It went on and on like that with Sari running back and forth trying to slap the ball away or tag the kid who was holding it. After a while we were running so fast and playing so hard that we forgot where we were and got closer and closer to where the old woman was sitting. Jessica took a throw from Gabe, and Sari saw her looking toward me. Sari ran in my direction, hoping to get to the ball before I did. Jessica flung it. It went wide, seemed impossible to catch, but I took off after it. At the last second, I jumped way up and reached for the ball with my left hand. I jumped so high, I felt like I was flying, and with a last stretch of my fingertips, I caught the ball.

Then it happened. I landed off balance, took two steps backward, tripped over the old woman's black shopping bag, and fell right on top of the red one.

For a moment, I didn't move. No one moved. The kids were all staring at me, waiting to see what I would do, what she would do to me. I was dazed, sitting in the midst of the spilled groceries and a dozen broken eggs. Then I saw her face. She was so mad, she looked like she wanted to murder me. I was so scared. I yelled out, kind of, and then I scrambled up and almost tripped again. I began running full speed toward the other kids. They all turned, ran for the gate, and waited for me there.

"Jon! What are you doing?" Jessica shouted.

It was a good question. I had no idea what I was doing. I had stopped and was looking back toward the old woman. I turned to Jess when she called to me, but I didn't say anything, and then I began walking back to where the old woman was bent over her bags.

"Let me help," I said, and bent down to where she was.

"Leave me alone," she snapped, almost snarled. "I don't need no help. This is your help," she said, pointing to the smashed and splattered eggs. "I don't need no help. Stupid kids," she said. "Stupid kids."

She grabbed her shopping bags and began hurrying, almost running toward the gate, toward where the rest of them were standing. I could see that the kids were terrified, and they nearly fell over each other getting out of her way. She didn't do anything, though. She just marched through the gate and turned under the El toward the neighborhood a few blocks away.

We didn't say anything at all as we walked together in the other direction under the El, but when we came to my corner, everybody stood for a bit, waiting.

"You okay, Jon?" Jessica finally asked.

"Yeah, I'm fine," I said. "I'll be fine. See you guys." I waved and turned up my street, and they all continued on under the tracks. I wasn't fine, though. In a few moments I was back at the corner. I looked after my friends and saw that they were already a block and a half away. Then I looked in the other direction. I saw no one, but I began walking that way, slowly at first and then more quickly. When I rounded the curve where the street bent to the right, I could see her way in the distance, and I followed her into her neighborhood, watching to see where she would turn in, where she lived. If I could just give her back the eggs, I thought, then maybe I wouldn't have this awful feeling about it—maybe it would be all right.

Her neighborhood and mine were very different, and even though they weren't far apart, I had never seen these streets before. We never went there; it wasn't our neighborhood. Where I lived, there were tall apartment buildings with grass and some trees between them. Here there was no grass and only a few trees. The buildings were all low, three or four floors, and most of them had a small store on the ground floor. I passed by a few grocery stores, many of them bodegas, or Latino grocery stores. I saw an automatic laundry, a few bars, one small synagogue, and lots of churches. There were lots of people on the street, and I recognized some of the kids from school. But I kept my eye on the old woman and saw her turn into a doorway next to one of the bodegas. I walked toward the small building. I felt nauseous as I got nearer, and I started to sweat. I wondered if I was going to be sick. I stood looking at the door for a moment, and then I went into the store.

"Yes, my friend? What can I do for you?" The owner of the bodega had a round brown face, shiny black hair, and a mustache. He was smiling.

"A dozen eggs, please." I paid him with my hot fudge sundae money. I remember wondering if it was worth it.

"You're not from around here, yes?"

"Yes. I mean no, I'm not," I answered, clutching the brown paper bag, but I didn't move.

"Is there something else I can do?"

"No. No, thank you." I turned to leave, but I stopped at the door and turned back. "The old lady . . . I mean the woman . . . with the black and red bags. Where does she live? I mean what apartment?"

"You mean Mrs. Rosenberg? She lives on the top floor, rear apartment." He leaned over the counter until his face was inches from mine. "You going to rob her?"

"No, no—I just want to—I mean I have to . . . these eggs . . ."

"It's okay, amigo," the man said. "I'm just joking. Go ahead. Top floor in the back."

I smiled a half smile. Some joke, I thought, and left the store. When I got outside, I just stood there looking at the door, wishing I hadn't come, thinking I would turn around and go home after all. Then a car horn beeped and I jumped. I reached for the building's door handle and went in.

It was dark inside. There was only one dim lightbulb in the hallway, and most of the lights on the staircases were out. I started up. I was biting my lip so hard that it bled. The steps creaked. I tried to place my feet more and more softly, but the noise of the steps just seemed to get louder and louder. I grabbed hold of the banister, and it wobbled. Halfway up to the first floor, I just fell down, like my legs couldn't hold me. I landed on my right elbow, managing to keep the eggs in my left hand from hitting the floor. I pulled myself up and went on. I started to get used to the dim light and even the creaking steps, but I tiptoed past each of the apartments. I really didn't want anyone to hear me. Somebody did and yelled out, "Who's there?" from behind one of the doors. I didn't answer—just hurried on. The last flight up was pitch-black. Finally I reached the fourth landing—the top. My heart was pounding and I was out of breath, and not because it was that many steps.

I turned to walk toward the rear apartment. I blinked hard twice, trying to adjust to the dark, but then I realized that it wasn't so completely dark after all. There was, in fact, a kind of a light—a green, sickening light. I saw the 4R on the door. The R was askew, hanging from one nail at the bottom. Then I saw her. Mrs. Rosenberg, the old woman, was lying there, twisted over and under her bags. The key was in the door, but the door was still locked. Her eyes were open and her mouth was open, her lips peeled back over her teeth. I couldn't take my eyes off her teeth. They were yellow and rotten, and some of them were gone. Then I looked back at her eyes, and they were wide open but empty, like they couldn't see. She was dead. I knew she was dead, and I yelled.

But then I saw that light again—that pale, green light—and I gagged. It was coming from her mouth, like a fog rising up out of her. I followed it with my eyes as it rose over her horrible face. At first, I just stared, not recognizing what it was. But then I saw it for what it was, saw that it was looking at me with those same wide open eyes. Not empty, though, but red like fire and filled with hate. That same mouth, but writhing and hissing and wanting something—wanting me! It was floating in thin air! A ghost! It was a ghost! Her ghost! I screamed and screamed and screamed, staring at that horrible green ghost, but I was paralyzed.

Then one of its hands reached for me, and finally I could move. I jumped back. I tripped over myself and banged my face on the railing and then I pulled myself up and ran, half falling down the stairs. I smashed into the storekeeper on the way down. He must have heard the screams and was running to see. I looked up at him and held on to him and tried to say something, but my lips were trembling and my teeth were clattering. I twisted free and ran away, down the stairs. Halfway down, I tripped again and tumbled the rest of the way to the ground floor. I jumped up and burst through the door, running, running all the way home.

That night at home, it was as though I were in some other place or somebody else's body. I heard everything that my family said, but I paid no attention. And they talked about me like I wasn't there.

"He's been like this ever since I got home," my mom said to my dad when he got home. "He just sits there in the middle of his bed, legs crossed, and doesn't say a word. He stares, he shakes, and sometimes he sobs. He won't answer me. He hardly looks at me."

"Jonathan!" Dad shouted, "Jonathan! Talk to me!"

I didn't. I didn't speak, I didn't eat, I didn't do anything. Mom and Dad didn't stop talking to me and asking me all kinds of questions. They coaxed and pleaded and yelled, but I just sat there.

"There's something very wrong here," Dad finally said. "It's not going to go away."

Dad was right. They put me to bed. I let them lay me down and pull the blanket up under my chin. I held the blanket to me, scrunched up, the way I did when I was little. They kissed me and turned out the light, but they left the door to my room open and the foyer light on. Holding tight to my blanket, with Mom and Dad in the next room, I began to feel a little safe and a little sleepy. Somehow, I fell asleep.

But in the middle of the night, she came for me. In my own house. In my own room. That sickening green light woke me up. She hung there, reaching with those hands, those long fingers and raggedy fingernails. I pressed my back up against the headboard, wishing I could get through it and through the wall behind it. I held my hands up in front of me, but I knew they couldn't keep her away. I screamed as she began to come across the bed for me. She almost touched me. She was about to take hold of me when Mom and Dad rushed through the door and she disappeared. I stopped screaming. I saw Mom and Dad where she had been just a second before. I blinked, and blinked again, but she was gone. And then I crawled across the bed, reaching for my dad and my mom. I grabbed hold of them, squeezing them to me, and I cried the way I had when I was tiny and wanted my mommy. And I cried because I was afraid and cold and I had no hope. I cried for more than an hour, always clutching my parents to me, first one, then the other. I told them everything and they held me tight, their tears mixing with my own. Finally I fell asleep, exhausted, still holding them.

They stayed with me all night, but I don't think they slept.

In the morning, the three of us sat around the breakfast table. I took just a little sip of juice and didn't touch my oatmeal. Mom and Dad drank lots of coffee.

"Jonathan, listen to me." Dad said. I hated it when he talked to me like that, like I didn't know anything. "It was a dream, Jonathan. You feel bad because you broke the old woman's eggs. She died, Jonathan, because she was old and sick, not because of the eggs. It's understandable that you would feel bad, but Jonathan, you didn't see a ghost. One more time, Jon—there are no ghosts."

I argued with them a bit, but of course it was no use. I could never convince them I had seen a ghost, and for sure they couldn't convince me that I hadn't. So I just shut up. I was crazy.

"We're going to find someone for you to go and see. Someone to help you," Mom said at the end of it all.

"Whatever," I said. "Whatever you want. I'll go to a shrink." I was so mad at them. They wouldn't believe me. "But I'm telling you—I saw a ghost. Mom, Dad, I saw a ghost and the ghost wants me. The ghost hates me." When I said those last words, I remembered it all again. I stopped being angry and just felt scared.

~

So I saw a shrink, Dr. Andrew Donovan, every day that week. He was very nice, but he didn't believe me. "Have you always had an active imagination, Jon?" he asked that first time. "Lots of people see things that seem very real to them," he observed. "Do you ever think about hurting yourself?" None of it made any sense or any difference, but I kept on seeing him every day because I couldn't think of anything else to do. I also kept on seeing Mrs. Rosenberg.

She came to me only at night and only when I was alone. She always had that same horrible, green light. She was always reaching for me, and her mouth was always open, always showing her rotten yellow teeth. I would see her and scream and scream until someone heard and shouted, or came into the room, and then she would disappear.

She always reached for me, but she touched me only once. I must have been more exhausted than usual that night because all the other times, it was the green light that woke me up. This time I stayed asleep until I felt one clammy finger slipping off the collar of my pajama top and sliding on to the skin of my neck. Her touch woke me, but for a second I didn't realize what it was. Then I opened my mouth to scream, but this time no sound came out. I ran for the door, but she was there first. I picked up things to throw at her. I flung a football, flung my Statue of Liberty paperweight, but they went right through her. I jumped over my desk chair and shoved it at her, but she passed through it and came at me again. There was nothing I could do, nowhere I could go.

I panicked and I think my heart stopped. I ran for the window, tried to open it, but it was stuck. I started smashing my fist against it. I banged it once, banged it again, and the glass shattered. This seemed to stop her. She just looked at me. I caught a glimpse of myself and realized I was bleeding from my knuckles and from farther up my arm, and I felt blood dripping down into my left eye from somewhere on my forehead. A shard of flying glass must have cut me. The ghost did something I hadn't seen before: she closed her mouth, and her eyes paled.

"Jonathan!" Dad cried, as he burst through the door, and the ghost disappeared.

"Jonathan!" Mom cried. She saw the broken window, and then she saw her son and his bleeding hand and face. "Oh, my God!" she said, and ran to me.

"Watch your feet, Susan," Dad said. They were both barefoot, and the floor was covered with glass. "Here, let me brush some of it away. . . . Jonathan," he said again after a few moments when most of the glass was off the floor and we could walk out of the room, down toward the kitchen. "Jonathan, what happened?"

I looked at my father, then at my mother, and then back at my father. I tried to say something, but then I stopped. "Nothing, Dad," I finally said. "Nothing happened. I . . . had a dream. A bad dream. You were right, Dad."

"But the window. . . ."

"Nothing happened, Dad," I said and I wouldn't say any more about it.

~

Things changed after that night, for me and for her. She kept on coming, maybe even more than before, but she never again went after me. She didn't even reach for me. She just appeared and looked at me. It was like she was searching for something. Lots of times she opened her mouth as if to speak, but she never said anything.

As for me, I wasn't so afraid anymore. Either I didn't think she was going to kill me, or I didn't care. That was it, really. I just wasn't interested in living. I ate less and less because nothing tasted good to me. I only went through the motions with schoolwork, and I stopped doing homework altogether. I spent no time with my friends and even avoided Jessica. Mom and Dad were going crazy themselves. They saw what was happening to me, and they couldn't do anything about it.

I wandered the neighborhood. I had no destinations in mind; I just walked. Mostly, I walked back and forth under the El. One time, I walked over to the park where it had all started. It was empty. The kids didn't go there any more, and no others had taken our place. I half expected to see the old woman sitting on her bench, but Mrs. Rosenberg wasn't there and neither was her ghost.

Finally Rosh Hashanah came. Despite everything, I had sort of been looking forward to it. I think I hoped, somehow, that it would make a difference. It didn't, though. Not at first. I sat in the synagogue with my father on my right and my mother on my left, like always, an open book in my hand. I had always liked *shul* on the High Holy Days. I liked the special melodies of the different services. I liked the packed room and the confused swaying back and forth and the people singing separately and together at the same time. This year, I thought maybe God would help me. Maybe God would bring me comfort, or answers, or something. But nothing happened. I was distracted, couldn't concentrate. The teaching of the rabbi made no sense to me. The melodies of the cantor seemed foreign, yet I knew they were the same ones I had always heard. I was sweating and fidgeting, unable to sit still. Finally I had had enough and stood up to leave, to run away. But as I stood up, so did everyone else. Why were they doing this to me? Why wouldn't they let me go? I was ready to scream.

"*Tekiah . . .*" The cantor's voice called out, followed by the blast on the shofar, the ram's horn.

I straightened up and looked at the rabbi, blowing the shofar. There was no more fidgeting. No more sweating.

"*Shevarim . . .*" called the cantor, and the one long blast was broken into three shorter ones. "*Teruah . . .*" and the blast of the shofar was shattered, splintered into pieces. My chest was rising and falling and I could hardly catch my breath.

"*Tekiah gedolah . . .*" The blast was put back together, long and clear and mighty.

I looked down at the prayer book, open by chance to a page I had not chosen in the middle of the service. "On Rosh Hashanah it is written and on Yom Kippur it is sealed . . . who will live and who will die . . . who by fire and who by water . . . who will be disturbed and who will be at rest." My hands holding the book trembled, and my eyes filled with tears.

On Rosh Hashanah it is written, I thought, and on Yom Kippur it is sealed. I looked farther down the page. "*Teshuvah, tefillah, tzedakah . . .* Penitence, prayer, and charity will avert the severe decree." I almost cried out. "I have to go, Mom," I said, and got up to leave.

"But Jon . . ."

"It's okay, Dad. I'm okay." I left the *shul*.

I wasn't wandering, though. I went straight to her neighborhood, straight to her door, and stood in front of the bodega. I walked into the store just as I had on that other day.

The storekeeper was handing a paper bag to a young mother, who put the package in her shopping bag behind her baby's stroller.

"*Gracias,* señora," he said, and as he said it, he noticed me standing there. He rushed out from behind the counter, still looking at me, and held the door for the woman.

"*Gracias,*" she said.

"*De nada,*" he said. "*Hasta mañana.*" He turned toward me and wiped his hands on his apron. "Is that you?" he asked. "You look so . . . are you all right?"

"I . . ." I didn't know what to say, and he waited.

"Yes?" he finally asked.

"I don't know. I'm not sure why I came here."

The man shrugged as if to say he didn't know either.

"What happened to her?"

"She died. You did not know that? I thought you knew. She was already dead when you. . . ."

"I know that. That's not what I mean. What happened after that?"

"First tell me your name. I'm Santiago." He reached out his hand.

"Jonathan. Jonathan Robbins." I shook the man's hand. That felt good.

It was the first thing in all that time that felt good. "Now tell me. Please?"

"What's to tell? It was horrible. I felt very bad, like I was responsible. Like I. . . ."

"What do you mean?" I interrupted. "Did you . . . did she . . . I mean did you have any reason?"

"Well, I usually, if I saw her. . . I would go out and carry her bags for her. Up the stairs, I mean. But that day it was busy in the store. I saw her, but I let her go. If I could have. . . if I would have just. . . ." He was remembering, and regretting all over again.

"But that's all? She didn't. . .?"

"That's all." Santiago looked at me with a question on his face. "What do you mean?"

"Nothing. Nothing." I paused for just a moment, and then I asked, "Is she buried?"

"Of course. What else? They wouldn't just leave her there."

"Where? How?"

"Oh, well . . . let me tell you. You feel bad for her, don't you, amigo? Let me tell you. It is sort of a nice story." Santiago waited, gathering those other memories. "I called 911, and the police came and took her to the morgue, to the medical examiner. When someone dies at home, the medical examiner must be called. But after she was gone, I couldn't stop thinking about it, about her. Also about you. I wished I knew who you were. I wished I could find you. Anyway, I had an idea. I closed the store and I walked over to Thirty-fifth Street, to the little synagogue. I knew she was Jewish, so I thought maybe some Jewish place should know she had died. It was a good idea. The rabbi, Rabbi Goldstein, knew just what to do. He called this organization—here, I have the name—" He reached behind the counter and felt around until he found a small business card. "The Hebrew Free Burial Association. They give a Jewish burial, free, for any Jewish person who dies without money for a funeral. They went and got her body from the morgue, and they took care of her in some special way, the way Jewish people are supposed to, I guess, and they buried her in their cemetery on Staten Island. I went. A person should not be buried with no one. So she's buried. Without a proper marker, maybe, but at least with her own people." Santiago finished his story, and the two of us were quiet.

"That was nice. Nice of you, I mean."

Santiago shrugged.

After a few moments, I straightened up and looked at him. I had thought of something. "Mr. Santiago," I asked, "do you need help?"

"What do you mean?"

"In your store, I mean. I mean, could you use somebody to help around here?"

"You want a job?"

"Yes. Do you have one for me?"

"I . . . don't think so. Why?"

"I just thought . . . are you sure?"

"It's a small store. There's not much to—wait a minute. Maybe you could deliver."

"Yeah, I could do that."

"My wife makes these empanadas, these meat things wrapped in dough. They're delicious. Everybody loves them and always asks for them, but I can't get them to them. Maybe you could. The people would call during the day, and you could deliver them before supper."

"That's perfect."

"Not so perfect. The people want them, and my wife can make them, but I have very little to pay you."

"Oh," I said, and the excitement died. "Wait a minute. It's not a problem. I'll just work for the tips. Is that okay?"

"It's okay with you?"

"Sure."

"Then it's good for me. It's a deal." We shook hands. "And if it works out, and it really makes some money, then I'll pay you, too."

"Great. Can I start tomorrow?"

"Tomorrow is fine."

"Great. I'll see you tomorrow. Thanks a lot, Mr. Santiago."

"You're welcome," Santiago said, but I was already out the door.

~

So I worked for Mr. Santiago, delivering Mrs. Santiago's very delicious empanadas. Business was good, and the tips were good. After a while, Santiago paid me a small salary, and I saved all the money, since I never did anything and had nothing to spend it on. I still saw Mrs. Rosenberg's ghost, and it was a constant fear, but I got used to it. It was like being a little sick all the time, but I learned to live with it because I thought now that I could do something about it. I hardly even looked at her anymore. I knew she would disappear if anyone else was present, so as soon as I knew she was around, I would find someone else to be with. I didn't notice the changes in her. Forgetting my own fear, I didn't see the growing fear and despair in her green and ghostly face. The months were passing. The money was piling up. The thing was getting done, and I was making it get done.

~

Finally the year had come around again. Rosh Hashanah services, which a year earlier had started this thing I was doing, were just great. The shofar calls were blasts of hope and even triumph. Everything was ready. Everything was in place. I was sure.

A week later on a Sunday afternoon, the eve of Yom Kippur, our red minivan turned in through the gate of Mount Richmond Cemetery on Staten Island, the cemetery of the Hebrew Free Burial Association. It was raining hard, and it was cold and very windy. We pulled up behind a white Buick, the only other car in sight, next to the one small, run-down gray building. I got out, followed by Mom, Dad, and Jessica. The cold rain, soaking me through almost immediately, made me wonder, made me a little less sure. When he saw us, Mr. Santiago got out of his Buick, and just seeing him made me feel better again. I ran to him and shook his hand. "Thanks for coming," I shouted over the howling wind.

"Of course," Santiago answered.

"Who are you?" Dad asked him.

"Felix Santiago. Jonathan works for me." He held out his hand, but Dad ignored it.

"Works for you? What is this? Susan, do you know anything about this?"

Mom shook her head.

"Jonathan," Dad shouted, but I had already begun looking among the graves.

"Do you know where it is, Mr. Santiago?" I yelled, feeling at a loss among hundreds of gravestones, in the midst of the driving rainstorm.

"No, Jonathan. I'm sorry. I cannot remember."

"Come on, then. I'll try and count." And I motioned for them to follow me.

The rain was harder now, and it was beginning to mix with sleet. It was only two o'clock, but overcast as the day was, it already seemed dark. I led them up one path and then back down it. I turned right and then left, counting, searching. I got up on my tiptoes, trying to see over the hundreds of graves with their stones piled up almost one on top of the other. The slashing wind made our umbrellas useless. We were all drenched now.

"Do you know where you're going?" Dad shouted over the wind. "Jonathan!"

"He's looking for something, David. Let him find it," said Mom.

"Here it is," I said. "Over here." I was standing next to a partly covered gravestone. The grave itself had nothing growing on it except some weeds, and the dirt was all mud in the midst of the storm. The cheesecloth covering, placed by the cemetery or perhaps the monument company, was mostly washed off the stone, but it still hid the carved writing.

"All right, Jonathan, we're here and you found it," said Dad. "Now what? What is this all about? We're soaked and freezing."

"Jon," Jessica asked, "Is this her?"

"Yes."

"I don't understand. Why are we. . . ."

"I'll tell you, Jess. I'll tell all of you." I was looking down at the ground, trying to figure out where to start. "Dad . . . Mom . . . this is that old woman. The one with the shopping bags. On that last day when we played in the park, and I broke her eggs—"

I stopped, not knowing how to continue, but they were all quiet, waiting for me.

"When I broke the eggs, and when she said those things to me—'stupid kids,' she said—I felt horrible. I followed her home to replace her eggs. That's when I met Mr. Santiago. I bought the eggs in his store. I found out what apartment she lived in and I went upstairs. I was scared to see her alive, but when I saw that she was dead, I just stood there shivering. And then I saw . . . I know you don't believe this . . . I saw her ghost. It was like a green smoke that came out of her mouth, and she hated me. She reached for me."

"Jonathan, not again."

"But Dad, please. Maybe I didn't see a ghost. Maybe I'm really crazy, but I'm not making it up. I really think I saw it, and I've seen it over and over and over again, and I didn't know what to do. Nobody could help me."

"Oh, Jon, I'm—"

"I'm sorry, Mom. I'm sorry, Dad, but nobody could help me. Not you. Not you, Jess. Not Dr. Donovan. And I had to stop seeing her. So finally I had this idea. It came to me, or it started to come to me, last year on Rosh Hashanah, when I heard the shofar. If I could do something to make up for it, maybe she would leave me alone. I didn't know for sure why, but that's why I went back to her neighborhood, to her building. It's why I went back into your store, Mr. Santiago. And then when you told me about her burial and that there wouldn't be any special marker, then I knew that's what I wanted to do. I thought . . . so I asked Mr. Santiago for a job, and he gave me one. I saved all my money and I bought this stone. It's an unveiling, Dad, like we had for Grandpa."

"Jonathan, you did this?" Dad asked. He seemed amazed. He crouched down so his face would be on a level with mine. "Oh, my God, Jon, what a thing you've done." He was crying and had trouble speaking through his tears. "Do you know what a mitzvah, what a precious, good deed this is? The highest, Jonathan. Susan, do you know what a boy we have? And tonight is Yom Kippur! I'm so proud, Jonathan." He grabbed me and squeezed me to him.

I pushed gently away. "Dad, what am I supposed to do?"

Dad got up and stood next to Mom and Mom motioned for Jessica and Mr. Santiago to join them. All four of them were looking at me, and I stood alone by the stone. The rain and the wind made the only sound.

"Just take the veil off, Jon," Dad said.

As I reached for the cheesecloth, the wind died and the rain now fell straight down. I pulled the torn and flimsy veil away.

HERE LIES
GITTEL ROSENBERG
DIED SEPTEMBER 17, 2001
FORGIVE ME

The five of us stood together in the deepening darkness, looking at the inscription.

" 'Forgive me,' Jonathan?"

"I know, Dad. You're not supposed to talk *to* the person in the writing on the stone. You're supposed to talk *about* her. The stonecutter told me. But

I had to say it, and I was too scared to talk to her ghost."

"Pick up a pebble, Jonathan," Mom said, "and put it on the stone." I reached down and found a smooth, reddish pebble and placed it on the gravestone, near the center.

"May I?" asked Santiago.

"Of course," said Dad. "All of us." Each one now bent and found a small rock or pebble and set it near mine. Dad put his arm around me. I hugged him, then Jessica and then Santiago, and finally Mom.

Mom kissed me and wiped the tears from my eyes and from her own. "Let's go home," she said. We turned toward the cars, but before we had gone even a few steps, I stopped in my tracks. There was the sickly green reflection on the monuments in front of me.

"Oh, no," I said. "No!" and I turned to face it.

She was there, hovering over her grave, plain now for all to see. Her eyes were wide, not lit, and almost empty, desperate. Her mouth was open, but there were no teeth. It was Gittel Rosenberg, but it hardly looked like her any more.

"Nooo!" I screamed. "Go away! Leave me alone. I'm sorry. I'm sorry. I can't do anything else. Leave me alone. Oh, please leave me alone." I sank to my knees, sobbing.

"Jonathan . . ." It said my name. "Jonathan . . ."

I said nothing now. I had no words. Only a sound, a long, drawn-out sound over and over again—a shriek of hopelessness, louder and louder. She came toward me, hanging there, inches from my face.

But now Dad and Mom were there, standing between the ghost and me.

"Leave him!" they shouted. "Leave! Go away!" And Dad rushed at the ghost, leaping and somehow grabbing onto it. He reached for her neck, and seemed surprised even as he did it that there was any real neck to grab. "Leave my boy alone!"

At that there was a horrible wail from the ghost, and a huge, powerful wind whirled around her and me, tearing Dad's hand off from her neck and separating the ghost and me from Mom and Dad. My parents struggled to get through, but they couldn't. I could see them screaming, but I couldn't hear them.

"Mommy . . . Daddy . . ." My voice now was weak and almost spent. "Mrs. Rosenberg," I said, crying, "I'm sorry. Why can't you forgive me? Why can't you?"

It reached a long, crooked hand for me and covered over my mouth. I stared into those terrifying, empty eyes.

"Forgive you?" it said. "Forgive you for what? What have you done? No, Jonathan, don't speak. There is no time. Let me. In my life, my wasted life, I never could speak. Now I have only one moment left. One moment before . . . I must speak now, or . . . please, Jonathan, listen. Forgive you? No, Jonathan. You have done nothing. It is you who must forgive me, though I have brought you nothing but fear and torment. Can you forgive me?"

"For what?"

"For my words. For my evil thoughts. Jonathan, you broke my eggs. For broken eggs, I damned you. There was anger in my heart for nothing. I died bitter and hateful and so I will be until the end of time, God forgive me, unless—oh, Jonathan, but God cannot forgive me—only you can forgive me. Can you forgive me, Jonathan, for those words, for my cold and bitter heart?"

The wind was howling again, and it seemed that the tombstones themselves were shaking. The pale, green light began to shimmer.

"Can you, Jonathan?" and there was terrible urgency and a horrible fear in her voice.

"Forgive you? But—"

"Can you? Will you, Jonathan? Please . . . please . . ."

The form of the old woman began to break up, dissolving in the swirling wind.

"Mrs. Rosenberg, I—I don't—"

"Jonathan . . . Jonathan . . ." With each word now, the voice became louder, more shrill, more frightened and farther away. "Jonathan . . ."

"Yes! Yes, Mrs. Rosenberg. I forgive you."

"Yes? Yes? Oh, Jonathan, yes!"

She spoke the final yes with love and great thanksgiving, and the wind and rain stopped. The pale, green light turned white, sparkled into a thousand bright stars, and disappeared.

~

I stared at the place where the stars had been and then realized that the four others were with me. "Come, Jonathan," Mom said, "Let's go. It's over."

I held back and looked once more at the gravestone. The clouds had broken up, and it was lighter. A mist—a regular mist of the world—hung over the stone for a moment, and then a gust of wind blew it away, showing us the inscription again. "Look, everybody," I said. "Look!" The inscription had changed.

HERE LIES
GITTEL ROSENBERG
DIED SEPTEMBER 17, 2001
FORGIVEN.

~ Background Note from the Author ~

I wrote this story in part because I was delighted to be asked to contribute to this collection. Many of my stories touch on inter-generational themes, specifically the difficulty that children and the elderly sometimes have communicating with each other and the moving power that such communication has when obstacles are overcome. Of course, death is a daunting obstacle, but the idea of a ghost story nevertheless appealed to me greatly. I'm interested in souls, perhaps because I officiate at many funerals and spend rather more time in cemeteries than most. Sometimes, I think, I even enjoy the company of the dead.

~ About the Author ~

JERRY RAIK was born and raised in New York City. He is a story-teller and the longtime director of the Havurah School, a program in after-school Jewish education through the arts. He lives on the Upper West Side of Manhattan with his wife, Barrie, and his three children: Rebecca, Joseph, and Molly.

Mrs. Samson Is Upstairs

~ Susan Stone ~

It was the year of my twelfth birthday—1966—and boy did I get a good haul that year! Almost everything I wanted: a Barbie doll from Aunt Nancy (even though I was officially too old); a leather vest with fringes that was much too big, given to me by my older sister; a really cool yellow portable radio from Grandma Sylvia , so small I could hold it in my hand; and silver dollars from my Grandma Rose. My parents gave me a pink jewelry box with a mirror on the inside reflecting a beautiful ballerina, who turned to music when the box was opened.

Still, I wished I had a mohair sweater like my sister's . . . or a trip to the beauty parlor to get my hair straightened. Or . . . well, my parents said I was never happy with what I had. But I was! It's just that, well, it seemed that I never had as much as . . . Barbara Samson, for instance. She was a friend in my seventh-grade class at school.

My birthday coincided that year with Shavuos. My mom was making cheese blintzes and homemade chunky applesauce that looked like someone had puked in a jar. And a birthday cake too, of course.

"Pepi, get your shoes on. We have to visit Mrs. Samson."

Mom and almost everyone else called me Pepi even though I was named Josefa, after my great-grandma. Mrs. Samson happened to be Barbara's grandma, but she was also a terrific seamstress. That afternoon, before *erev* Shavuous we went to visit old Mrs. Samson to pick up the special dress I was having shortened to wear at Barbara's upcoming Bat Mitzvah.

The apartment building itself was huge. Mrs. Samson owned it—she was rich, I suppose—but for some reason she chose to live in a tiny apartment on the second floor. On the first floor was Orchid Dry Cleaner's, and a cardboard sign written in red marker in its front window read: *Mrs. Samson Is Upstairs.*

So we *shlepped* up the steep steps, looking forward to the butter cookies, hot tea, and cool stories. Mrs. Samson greeted us cordially at the door. "Good afternoon, Mrs. Rosenfeld. Hello, Josefa. Please come in." The aroma of freshly baked cookies, lemon slices accompanying the tea, and slightly dusty old cushions all had a hypnotic effect on me, and I slipped into a bit of heaven on earth.

Stories, like chocolate syrup, flowed from Mrs. Samson sweetly and slowly; strange and glorious tales of her childhood in a small Hungarian village. But the best stories always involved goblins, bits of magic, and mysterious happenings in the dark woods near her home in the old country. "Let me tell you about the time, *mamele,* dear one, when my cousin Ignatz got his thumb caught in the pickle barrel on a night with a full moon, and no one could get it out until. . . ." Or, "There was a man named Yosele Teglasher who could throw a stone through a window and it wouldn't shatter—it would just make a little hole. . . ." I'll tell you those another time.

Yiddish phrases peppered her tales, and she always laughed at her own jokes. I laughed too, because she was so jolly, although I rarely understood the jokes. I felt a peace in Mrs. Samson's apartment that I never felt anywhere else. Warm. The way hot cocoa feels when it goes down your throat and warms you from the inside out.

It was as if I really was transported through time and space, like the time traveler in *The Time Machine*—to the women's section of the synagogue, for instance, or to the old kitchen to watch the dough being kneaded, or to the garden to pick cabbages. I "saw" the angels, the goblins, the old rabbis, and even, even, the Angel of Death!

"It came for my beloved husband, Sandor," Mrs. Samson sadly related. "It was a terrible sight. . . ."

This last tale was not so old. Sandor Samson had died only a year ago.

"I'm really sorry about Mr. Samson," I whispered respectfully.

"*Bubbe meises*—old wives' tales!" my mom muttered disdainfully under her breath.

Mrs. Samson continued. "We were sleeping soundly when I heard a rustling at the window. Scratching. Green fog seeped in at the windowsill, and I nudged Sandor.

"'Sandor. Please open your eyes. Please. Something's here. I can feel it.' The room grew cold and damp, and my Sandor didn't move." Mrs. Samson took an embroidered hankie from her apron pocket and dabbed at her nose.

"I couldn't move either," she whispered. "I just lay there clutching the covers to my chin and watched as the *Malach Hamaves,* the Angel of Death, with its thousand glaring eyes, sneaked up on him and . . ." Mrs. Samson choked up. Mama put a hand gently on her knee. "I couldn't help him, Mrs. Rosenfeld. There was nothing I could do but watch as the last breath was sucked out of him, may he rest in peace."

I sat on the lumpy green sofa with my tea and cookies while Mrs. S. composed herself, and in silence Mama and I watched her put the finishing touches on my dress. I would be the most fashionable girl at Barbara's Bas Mitzvah. Yeah, but somehow that didn't seem so important at the moment.

A side table, littered with framed photos of bearded men and of women in long dresses with flowered babushkas covering their heads stood next to me, and I placed my cup carefully on top of the crocheted white cloth. One silver frame, though, had a modern photo—I recognized Barbara. A shaft of sunlight streamed in from a window, lighting up the ancient, worn Persian carpet, giving it new life. I cautiously looked around, making sure there was no trace of green fog. All was quiet except for the rhythmic ticking of a clock. I tried on the new dress.

"It looks lovely, *kaynahora!*" exclaimed the old seamstress, warding off the evil eye lest it hear of earthly happiness and come to take it away. My own grandma had uttered the Yiddish incantation a million times over all of us. (When she spoke of our beauty; when she told us how we had grown; when she talked about our *simchas* as in, "She'll be graduating in June, *kaynahora.* . . . She's getting so tall, *kaynahora.* . . . Look at that gorgeous hair, *kaynahora!*") My mom simply smiled, nodded her approval, and excused herself to go to the bathroom.

Then it happened. "Oooooooow . . . oooooooow!" From outside we heard a dog howling mournfully, as if it was suddenly sad. "Ooooooow." The sunlight vanished. The Persian carpet looked old again. Putting her sewing in her lap, Mrs. Samson looked up. Softly she whispered, "The Angel of Death is back in town!"

Flitting around the apartment like an anxious parakeet, she grabbed the saltshaker from the kitchen table, took off the top, and poured an avalanche of salt into my pocket. Then she took a safety pin from her overcrowded strawberry pincushion and pinned it onto my blouse "for added protection." She hugged me to her, crushing me in the soft padding of her body—which always smelled like latkes. With my face distorted and smashed against her chest, I looked up to see a silver hand with an open eye in the middle—a *chamsa*—dangling from a chain on her fleshy neck, to ward off evil. The open eye stared at me, curious.

My mother emerged from the bathroom, unaware. "Come, dear, we have to go home. Thank you, Sarah." I glanced back at Mrs. Samson. We left.

The next morning I found myself walking up the impressive cement staircase of our synagogue when a dog howled in the distance. Looking around uneasily, I decided that, okay, dogs sometimes howl. So what? "Get a grip on yourself," I said under my breath.

Guess who was walking up the stairs next to us? Yep, Mrs. Samson herself! What a *co-eenk-e-dink* (this is my Dad's way of saying coincidence)! She didn't even seem to hear the dreadful howl. She trudged slowly, one step at a time, upstairs. Her hair, like stuck-together Rice Crispies—the same color, too—was crowned by a white, lace snowflake, bobby-pinned tightly in place. She wore, as always, a faded grass-green dress with puffy sleeves, trimmed in white lace, and worn black leather shoes tied with frayed laces. I wondered what she would wear to Barbara's Bas Mitzvah next week. Why doesn't she buy herself some decent clothes, I wondered. Why does she look like that? Mrs. S., I smiled to myself, was weird. In a good way, of course.

My family, Mrs. Samson, and I sat in the third row on the red woolen cushioned seats, amid the quiet chatter. I waved at Barbara and some other friends who were just coming in, but there were no more empty seats around us. Until services began I loved to try and catch bits and pieces of conversation, scattering like feathers in the wind. Two women sat behind me to my left. In hushed tones they spoke of Mrs. Samson's great wealth and her frugality, her stinginess. "That Sarah Samson won't part with a penny," the skinny one sniped. I hoped it wasn't true. "Have you heard her muttering to herself in Yiddish?" the beehive-haired lady added. That part was true.

I glanced to my right to see if Mrs. Samson had overheard, but she was engrossed in the *siddur,* and I had no more time to ponder the gossip because services started.

We had been singing and praying for some time when the rabbi began, in Hebrew and in English, to recite the Ten Commandments as he did every Shavuos. The first few were all positive—what we *should* do—but the last five were suggestions, well, more than suggestions, about what we should *never* do. "Thou shall not murder. . . . thou shall not steal. . . . thou shall not covet. . . ." "Dad," I leaned to my left and whispered, "What does 'covet' mean?" "When you covet, Pepi," he whispered back, "you want something that someone else has."

That was it! I was relieved. Mrs. Samson wasn't a miser, like they said. She was just a person who didn't covet. A noncoveter. A covet-free person. A covetless person. She was happy with what she had! A small apartment and old clothes suited her just fine. She didn't have to "keep up with the Joneses" (or the Cohens).

The cantor began to lead us in a song, and I could hardly keep from staring at Mrs. Samson's three chins, which wobbled like Jell-O as she sang. Just when I almost choked from holding back the giggles, a chill came over me. "Why is it so cold in here, Dad?" I whispered. My dad did not respond. The air, like a frozen pond, didn't move. I could hear my parents, my sister, and all the others singing and mumbling their prayers. I could barely breathe. I heard "Thou shall not . . . " and then the lights dimmed as if a cloud had suddenly covered the sun outside.

Mrs. Samson's large figure pushed against my right arm and made my *siddur* jiggle every time she took a breath. It seemed as if Mrs. Samson and I were all alone and that no one else was making a sound. All I could hear was her sweet, high-pitched voice blending with mine like peanut butter and jelly as we sang and sang and sang. No one else was even moving. It was as if I was dreaming, but I'm telling you—it was real.

Then all of a sudden, a shadow like a gray ghost descended on Mrs. Samson, and green fog surrounded us. It was the Angel of Death! The gray form was covered with eyes, just as Mrs. Samson had described it. Green, bloodshot eyes from head to toe. I tried not to gape at all the eyes. If you did, I remembered, a drop of poison from its sword would fall into your open mouth. I knew it had come for old Mrs. Samson. "No!" I wanted to shout, all the while remembering to keep my lips tightly together. "Not yet!" The words stuck in my throat. Barbara wants her grandmother at her Bas Mitzvah! I heard myself thinking loudly, as if my head would burst.

I found myself standing on my chair, swinging and waving my siddur wildly in the air, swiping at the grisly presence. The chair wobbled along with Mrs. Samson's amazed countenance, and I heard myself mutter, softly at first, closing my eyes, "*Kaynahora, kaynahora.*" Then louder, "*Kaynahora. KAYNAHORA!* EVIL EYE AWAY!"

"I promise," I bargained with Whomever was listening, "I promise that I will try my hardest to be happy with what I have—not to covet anything— if Mrs. Samson can just live *one more week*." Opening my eyes, I swung that *siddur* as if my life depended on it, all the while hoping the holy letters would dissolve the unwelcome visitor into a wisp of a sigh, an ash, a yawn, a grain of sand.

Old Evil Eye would just have to wait. Wait? Who says? I say so, I thought. Like the creeping fog itself, another thought oozed its way into my head: Maybe, just maybe, if it didn't get Mrs. Samson it would turn and get me! For once in my life I didn't want what someone else had—the Angel of Death. Maybe it just wasn't my time, I hoped.

Suddenly I realized how lucky I was. I didn't want to die. I wanted to breathe and to laugh—and to go to college (first I wanted to visit Disneyland). I had so much—my family, friends, food, a house, love. I had me! Why did I waste energy always wanting what everyone else had? I already had what I really needed.

I began to mentally list my failings to see if I was really so bad that I would be next in line to die: I had once stolen a box of forty-eight crayons—oh! to have silver and magenta and aquamarine! But I did return it. My mom made me. I continued. . . . Once I found a key chain with a painted green turtle on a silver disc. Never even tried to find its owner. Then there was the time I lied and told my uncle that his jokes were funny—he smelled like moth balls and his jokes smelled worse, but I said they were funny, anyway. Maybe that wasn't so bad. But I knew always, always I broke the tenth commandment—I always wanted what I didn't have.

The list of my failings streamed through my head as I hoped that the dark shroud enveloping Mrs. Samson would not find reasons to turn itself on me. I shut my eyes tightly.

I wanted to save myself, sure, but mostly all I could think about was saving kind, funny old Mrs. Samson. My *siddur* whooshed through the air over and over, and I felt the Angel of Death retreating under the ferocity of my attack. My eyes opened and I stared at it intensely, forgetting the imminent danger. We looked eyeball to eyeball . . . to eyeball to eyeball. Trembling, I turned to Mrs. Samson.

"Chaya!" I yelled. "Chaya Esther! You look tired. Perhaps we should leave." I thought maybe if I addressed her by a different name, the Angel of Death, that shadowy figure, would think it had the wrong person. Mrs. Samson looked up at me, astonished, confused. The Dark Angel floated in my direction as if it had accepted that Mrs. Samson really was Chaya Esther, and it didn't want to make an appearance for nothing, so it came toward me. "*KAYNAHORA!*" I bellowed one last time. "EVIL EYE AWAY!!"

The specter faded away to nothing—along with the chartreuse fog. The lights returned to normal. I sighed. But people all around were staring at me, mouths open in disbelief. Mrs. Samson sat prim but shaken at the ordeal of having me, twelve-year-old Pepi Rosenfeld, waving a *siddur* wildly above her head. Neither she nor any of the others had seen the unholy visitor. She clutched her *chamsa.* My mother was tugging at my dress, to get me to sit down. "Close your mouths or you'll all die!" I shrieked at the onlookers, and sped out of the crowded sanctuary. I could feel more eyes on me— this time the eyes of hundreds of people watching me as I fled.

With my face buried in my hands, I sat on the front steps of the building crying, gulping for air, eyes swollen. I was exhausted. Even my usually wild curly hair lay limp down my back as if it, too, were tired and ashamed, and I was sure I had made a fool of myself.

As I wiped the back of my hand under my nose, someone from above handed down a tissue. Absentmindedly I took it and blew two *tekiahs* and one *tekiah gadolah* like shofar blasts. "Thanks," I whispered hoarsely. Slowly I tilted my head and looked up to see Mrs. Samson. (The tissue smelled like lavender, her special scent when she didn't smell like latkes.)

Mrs. Samson smiled sadly and several of her chins moved briefly to fold into one. Reaching up to straighten her collar, she then stood tall and swiped at a few beads of sweat on her upper lip.

"I felt so faint in there, Pepi," she said as she unpinned the lace doily from her Rice Crispies hair. "It was so stuffy. So warm. Thank you, *mamele,* for fanning some air in my direction. I feel better. Better. You shouldn't be embarrassed. They don't know from nothing. You did good. *Gey gezuntheit, mayn kind*—go in good health, my child."

"You're welcome Mrs. Samson," I croaked. Mrs. Samson slowly made her way down the front steps, one step at a time. I watched her gingerly confront each step as if she were descending Everest itself. Finally, when she reached the bottom, she looked up at me perched on the top step, smiled wanly, and pulled her dress downward from where it had crept. Clutching a small black leather purse under her ample arm, she carefully turned the corner, out of sight.

The last time I ever saw her was at Barbara's Bas Mitzvah the following week. She was beaming in a lovely green and beige plaid suit, doily on her head, the *chamsa* conspicuously missing from her neck.

I have never encountered the Angel of Death again, or any other angel for that matter, at least not so far. But Mrs. Samson did die. It was her time, I guess, and the Angel of Death visited her with compassion; several weeks later she died peacefully in her sleep. Mrs. Samson lived a good life; her memory was a blessing, at least to me.

Barbara came up to me a few weeks after her grandma's death and held out a small blue velvet box. "Here," she said as she thrust the box into my hand. "Here's what my grandma told me she wanted you to have." Her eyes looked sad, her braces shining behind her weak smile. On her neck was a silver chain on which dangled her grandma's *chamsa*. I recognized that eye (after all, we had been eyeball to eyeball). I was trying very hard to be glad to have whatever was in the blue box, but I have to admit that I wished I, too, had a necklace like Barbara's.

Later, finally at home in my own tiny room, I shut the door and abolished any remaining shadows in the room by turning on all the lights. I closed the windows, the curtains, the closet door. I looked under the bed. The checklist was complete—that multi-eyed apparition was nowhere to be found. With a bounce and a sigh I plopped down on my pink checkered bedspread and prolonged the anticipation by rubbing my cheek against the soft velvet box. Inside, on its blue velvet cushion, was a gleaming, silver *chamsa*—almost exactly like Mrs. Samson's!

Well, I'm very happy I'm alive and that the Evil One let me alone. Just like Mrs. S., I try to be happy with what I have. Barbara and I have become really good friends, *chamsa* sisters, we like to call ourselves, and we share each other's secrets. "My grandma," she whispered conspiratorially, "gave enough *tzedakah* to build a whole new wing of the Children's Hospital. But no one will ever know. She always said, 'Give, Barbara, for the sake of giving, not for what you'll get in return.'" I certainly won't tell. I wish my secrets were as interesting as hers (oops, there I go again).

One day we took the red-lettered sign out of the dry cleaner's window and took two different buses over to the cemetery where Mrs. Samson was buried. "It's over there," Barbara pointed, and we walked through tall grass, past several gray monuments with stars on them. A gentle breeze brushed our cheeks, and the sun showered us with warmth. There was no gravestone yet, just a marker, but we knew it was hers.

First we each placed a small stone on the earth and thought our separate thoughts. Then, like parents covering up a sleeping child, we gently laid the sign on top of her grave for all to read:

MRS. SAMSON IS UPSTAIRS.

~ Background Note from the Author ~

Like most people, I struggle with being satisfied with and appreciative of what I have. So when I chose the holiday of Shavuos as a beginning focus of the story, it was natural then that Pepi struggle with the commandment not to "covet." She's still struggling, as am I, but we're working on it. Many of the names and references in the story come from my own family or from stories I heard about Hungary, where my grandparents come from. I love the world of Jewish folklore: superstitions, weird happenings, the *yenne velt*—the other world, as they say in Yiddish. I remember hearing stories when I was young and sensing, even then, that things happen . . . that we can't explain.

~ About the Author ~

SUSAN STONE is a professional storyteller, weaving her tales for children and adults throughout the country. She performs multicultural stories and offers workshops and residencies at schools, museums, and storytelling festivals, but especially loves telling Jewish stories. She has performed them at religious schools, women's retreats, services, and private *simchas*. She has published two recordings for children, *The Angel's Wings: Jewish Tales from Around the World*, which won the Parents' Choice Gold Award, and her latest, *Feathers in the Wind and Other Jewish Tales*. She also has a story included in the book *Chosen Tales: Stories Told by Jewish Storytellers*. She has an M.A. in theater and has been a storytelling and drama teacher in many settings. Currently she is on the Illinois Arts Council Artstour Roster and the adjunct faculty of National-Louis University, teaching teachers to tell tales. Susan's husband and two children have been listening to her tales for a long time—Joel, Davida, and Avram (the names have been changed to protect against the Evil Eye).

The Shadow of the Golem

~ Malka Penn ~

Joey craned his neck back to check the time on the Jewish Town Hall. The clock at the top of the tower read five minutes after twelve. Beneath it, another clock showed the same time, only its hands pointed to Hebrew letters and ran counterclockwise.

"Grandma Mitzi's late for lunch, no matter what language the clock's in," Joey grumbled to himself, glancing again at his own watch.

He called it his old-new watch—old because it had once belonged to his Grandpa Joe, and new because it was a Bar Mitzvah gift from his grandmother, along with this trip to Prague. He didn't especially like the watch. It had to be wound every day, and he would have much preferred the latest digital model. But he decided it was no big deal to wear it for the week they'd be in Prague.

"Your grandfather would have been so proud of you," Grandma Mitzi had told Joey as she presented it to him on the long plane ride from Boston. "He never had a Bar Mitzvah ceremony himself. The war brought everything to a halt."

Joey had never met his grandfather, who had died a year before he was born. In spite of Grandma Mitzi's many stories about him, he never seemed quite real to Joey.

"You'll get to know him better by seeing where he grew up," she assured him.

Yet Joey felt no more connected to his grandfather now than he had before they arrived in Prague three days ago. It seemed all they had done was amble through narrow, cobblestoned streets, going from one tourist attraction to another. He was beginning to wonder if the trip wasn't more for his grandmother's sake than his.

Now, after a long morning of sightseeing, he was tired and hungry, waiting for his grandmother to come out of the Jewish Town Hall, where she was checking on afternoon tours.

"If I see one more museum . . ." Joey left his thought unfinished.

At that moment, Grandma Mitzi bustled out of the building, waving her hands.

"I found out today's last tour of the Old-New Synagogue is about to start."

"What about lunch?" Joey protested.

"We'll get it later. C'mon!" she shouted, and Joey had to run to keep up with her.

It was only a short block from the Jewish Town Hall to the Old-New Synagogue, but they arrived, out of breath, just as the tour guide was beginning her spiel.

"This is the oldest synagogue in Europe, built in 1270, and used continuously for over 700 years except from 1941 to 1945, during the Nazi occupation of Prague. . . ."

Immediately, Joey's mind wandered to his grandfather and the questions that had always haunted him. How did he survive the Holocaust in Prague? Where did he hide?

Every time he had asked Grandma Mitzi about it, she'd shrugged.

"He never said exactly where or how. He didn't like to talk about that terrible time."

The tour guide's voice brought Joey back to the present.

"According to legend, about four hundred years ago, Rabbi Loew, the leader of Prague's Jewish community, fashioned a giant creature from the mud of the Vlatava River. To bring this Golem, or shapeless thing, to life, he embedded the name of God in his forehead. The Golem then helped save the Jews of Prague from their enemies until one day he turned on them, too. So Rabbi Loew banished the Golem to the attic of this Old-New Synagogue, where, according to some, he still lives on."

Joey looked around the ancient synagogue, trying to picture the giant creature hanging out there. Instead of envisioning the Golem, however, he kept thinking about his grandfather. It was almost as if he could feel his presence.

"Did Grandpa Joe ever go to services here?" he whispered to Grandma Mitzi.

"Not that I know of, darling," she answered in her loud voice. "Most of the Jews moved out of this area long before he was born."

The people in front of them turned around with frowns and glares. Grandma Mitzi continued talking anyway.

"We can come back tonight for services, if you like," she said.

At that point, the tour guide was winding up her talk. "The Golem became the prototype for Frankenstein and other monster men," she concluded.

"Cool!" Joey responded to the tour guide's statement, not realizing he was also accepting his grandmother's invitation.

~

They arrived at the Old-New Synagogue late for the second time that day, descending the stairs to the crowded sanctuary as the opening prayers were being chanted. Grandma Mitzi was led to the far side of the room, behind a curtain with the other women. Joey took a seat in the back row of the center section with the men, who seemed to be mostly tourists like himself. He glanced at his watch. Seven o'clock on the nose. Another hour or so and they'd be out of there, he figured.

As he opened his prayer book, a drop of water splashed onto the pages.

"The old roof must be leaking," he whispered to the man sitting next to him.

The man was either deep in prayer or didn't understand English. In any case, he didn't respond.

Joey looked up, and more drops fell on his face. He brushed them off, tasting their saltiness, the taste of tears.

In that brief moment, it grew darker and quieter in the Old-New Synagogue. The man sitting next to him was no longer there. Neither, for that matter, was anyone else in his row, or in any of the seats in front of him. The curtain to the women's section was missing, revealing no one there either.

"Something weird's going on," Joey thought, curious and frightened at the same time.

A handful of men were gathered near the *bimah*—the pulpit. Rather than praying, they were speaking in low, excited tones. They seemed not to notice Joey at all, even when he moved closer to hear what they were saying.

Although they spoke in Czech, somehow it came out in English, like the voice-overs in those foreign films Grandma Mitzi was always dragging him to.

"We must thank God we are still here," an old man whispered in a trembling voice.

"How much longer will we be here? Maybe tonight they will come for you, or you, or you," a young man said, pointing to each man in the circle.

One of them waved his hand in disagreement. "They are just trying to scare us. We have survived other ordeals. We will get through this one, too."

The old man wrapped his prayer shawl more tightly around himself.

"If only the Golem were still alive," he sighed.

"A hundred golems couldn't save us now," the young man said. "We must each find a hiding place."

"First we must pray," the old man said. He began to sway back and forth, chanting the prayers. One by one, they all joined in. Then they left, also one by one, until Joey was all alone. He sat frozen for a few moments before he ran to the door after them.

It was locked, apparently from the outside. Frantic, he looked around for another exit. The only possibility was a narrow staircase leading up into darkness.

Now more frightened than curious, he climbed the steep stairs, pausing at each step to listen, but hearing only the pounding of his heart.

By the time he reached the top, he was immersed in darkness. Cautiously, he put his hand out. Feeling a wooden door directly in front of him, he groped for the knob. Though he barely touched it, hinges began to creak, and the door slowly swung open.

After his eyes adjusted to the dim light, Joey saw a large room piled with stacks of books all over the floor. A figure stepped out of the shadows and stood in front of him, a boy, about his age and height.

"You must hide here with us," the boy said. "He will protect you, too."

Joey gasped, not so much at the boy's words but at his face, which he could see more clearly now. It was as if he were looking into a mirror at a pale image of himself. His heart was pounding louder than ever.

"Who . . . who are you?" he asked the boy, although he had already guessed the answer.

"My name is Joseph. They came in the middle of the night and took my parents away. I had been staying at a friend's house, but it became too dangerous for his family to keep hiding me. I didn't know where to go. Then

I remembered the stories of the Golem my father had told me. I prayed he would still be here and help me. Only his Shadow remains, but it is enough." He paused. "Who are you?"

Joey considered saying, "I'm your grandson," but decided against it.

"My name's Joseph, too, but I'm called Joey," he finally said. "How long have you been here?"

"Almost four years."

"Four years! How do you get food?"

Joseph smiled faintly. "He accompanies me every night when I go out to scavenge. As long as I'm with him, I'm completely invisible. You see?"

As a demonstration, he stepped into the corner and disappeared in the shadows. After a moment, he stepped out again, turning back and speaking, as if to a small, unseen child.

"Don't be shy. Come out and meet someone else who believes in you."

There was a faint stirring, a flickering of lighter and darker shades of gray. Then, slowly, the outline of a giant man emerged as the Shadow of the Golem came forth. His head reached the ceiling before he lowered it to bow down to Joey.

"He doesn't speak," Joseph said, "but he is glad to see you. He has been very melancholy of late, sitting there crying in the corner."

"Then those were your tears!" Joey addressed the Shadow.

"They were," Joseph answered for him. "He thinks this terrible time will never pass. He weeps for all the Jews who have been killed. He is sorry he once turned against them."

The Shadow of the Golem began to quiver, and though he made no sound, Joey knew he was crying again. He tried to change the subject.

"How do you spend the days?" he asked Joseph.

"I tell him the stories my father told me about how the Golem helped the Jews of Prague long ago. He carried water and chopped firewood for them, and, more importantly, saved them from their enemies, who accused them of crimes they didn't commit.

"After a while, the Jews began to take the Golem for granted and forgot to thank him for helping them. They ignored him when they passed him on the street and acted as if he didn't exist."

Joey watched the Shadow of the Golem listening carefully, nodding his head, and clenching his fists as Joseph talked about how enraged the Golem had become from being neglected.

"Instead of carrying a few buckets of water, he emptied the whole Vlatava River into the streets of the Jewish quarter! Instead of chopping a cord or two of firewood, he cut down an entire block of houses! The people were very frightened, and banished him here to the attic of the Old-New Synagogue. Then Rabbi Loew removed the word of God from his forehead and told the people that the Golem had died."

Joseph paused. "But the Shadow of the Golem lives on, thank God."

Joey took a deep breath. He looked around the room at all the books.

Joseph answered his unspoken question. "This attic was a storage place for prayer books and other religious writings that could no longer be used. I wish I could read them, but I don't know Hebrew. I never had a Bar Mitzvah."

"I know," Joey said. "I mean, if you like, I could read them to you."

He picked up a large volume and walked over to the window where moonlight streamed through a broken pane. He opened the book at random and read a sentence in Hebrew before translating it.

"It says, 'If you save one life, it is as if you saved the world entire.'"

The Shadow of the Golem, who had resumed crying silently in the corner, stepped out again and bowed to Joey.

"He is grateful to you for having read that," Joseph said.

The moonlight was shining on Joey's watch.

"I like your watch," Joseph said. "When I get out of here, after all this is over, I want to get one just like yours."

Joey looked at the time on his watch.

"Twelve o'clock!" he exclaimed, surprised at the late hour.

"It is always midnight on the Jewish clock," Joseph said, pointing out the window.

Across the street, the moon shone on the tower of the Jewish Town Hall, lighting up the faces of its two clocks. Both sets of hands were pointing straight up. But when the clock at the top of the tower ticked to the right, one minute past midnight, the clock with Hebrew letters stood still.

"The Jewish clock stopped when the Nazis began their occupation of Prague," Joseph explained. "Of course they never fixed it. Anyway, it is time to go out and get some food. You must come with us."

Joey looked alarmed.

"Don't worry," Joseph told him. "You'll be under his protection."

The Shadow of the Golem led the way down the stairs and out the door of the Old-New Synagogue, which opened easily at his touch. Joseph walked on his left side, and Joey on his right, feeling scared and exhilarated at the same time as they passed group after group of Nazi soldiers without being seen or heard.

"If the Shadow of the Golem is protecting us, why can't we just run away to freedom?" Joey asked.

"I've tried many times to convince him, to no avail," Joseph said. "He won't set foot outside the Jewish quarter. It's been his only home for hundreds of years."

The two boys rummaged through garbage cans in front of the Jewish Town Hall as the Shadow of the Golem hovered over them. There was no food to be found there, and they continued down Maiselova Street, in and out of alleyways, also without success.

"Food has been getting scarce, but it has never been this bad," Joseph said.

When they came to the end of the street, they stopped.

"Isn't this where the Jewish quarter ends?" Joey asked.

"Yes," Joseph said. "I'm afraid I have no choice but to cross over into Old Town. You stay here with the Shadow of the Golem. I won't be long."

Joey stood by the Shadow's side and together they watched Joseph cross the street. It was completely deserted except for a cat creeping over the cobblestones. Then, just as the boy reached the other side, two Nazi soldiers turned the corner in his direction.

"Run, Joseph, run back to us," Joey shouted, realizing as he spoke that his words couldn't be heard.

But it was too late anyway. The soldiers had already spotted him. One of them grabbed his arms, while the other screamed at him in German.

Joey pleaded with the Shadow of the Golem.

"You must save him. You've protected him all these years. You can't lose him now."

The Shadow of the Golem didn't move.

"All you have to do is cross the street, and then come right back. I'll be with you."

The Shadow remained motionless. "Remember the words I read? 'If you save one life, it is as if you saved the world entire.' Well, you're not just saving Joseph's life, you're saving his children's lives and their children's lives. If you don't, I won't ever be born!"

The Shadow of the Golem looked puzzled. Then he began to tremble, a little at first, then more and more violently. Suddenly, he scooped Joey up in one arm, swept across the street, and while the soldiers looked around bewildered, lifted Joseph out of their grasp with his other arm.

Joey felt as if he were wrapped in a soft, warm blanket as the Shadow carried him and Joseph back through the streets of the Jewish quarter and up the stairs to the attic of the Old-New Synagogue.

They all collapsed into the corner, and for a long while no one said anything. Then Joey began to wonder what time it was.

He went to the window to read his watch in the moonlight. Twelve-thirty. Only half an hour had passed since they had left the attic in search of food, but it seemed like an eternity. He looked at the clock at the top of the Jewish Town Hall. It also said twelve-thirty. His eyes lowered to the clock with Hebrew letters, the one that had been stopped at midnight all these years. He blinked his eyes in disbelief.

"It's working! The Jewish clock is working!" he shouted.

Joseph ran to the window, and the two boys watched the clock tick to the left, again, and again, and again.

"It is a sign," Joseph said. "The war against the Jews is ending. The Allies will be here soon."

Joey took off his watch and handed it to Joseph.

"This is for you," he said. "To remember me by."

"But it's yours."

"It's okay," Joey said. "Someday I'll get one just like it."

He felt a hand on his shoulder and turned to find the Shadow of the Golem, who was crying silently.

"They are tears of relief, and also sadness, because we will be leaving soon," Joseph interpreted.

"I'm sorry," Joey said to the Shadow. "I wish I had something to give you, too. I only have my thanks, my deepest, deepest thanks."

The Shadow of the Golem continued crying, but Joey knew that now they were tears of joy.

~

The opening prayer was just concluding as Joey opened his eyes and checked his watch. Ten minutes after seven. He settled back, glad there was still almost an hour to go before the end of the service. For the first time, he realized that he was wearing his old-new watch in the Old-New Synagogue, and he smiled at the thought. He promised himself he would wear it every day for the rest of his life. Not that he needed a reminder of what had happened tonight. He could never forget that.

A drop of water fell on his prayer book.

"The old roof must be leaking," he whispered to the man sitting next to him. The man nodded in agreement.

Joey gently wiped off the drop of water and joined the rest of the congregation in singing praises to God.

~ Background Note from the Author ~

Both of my grandfathers died before I was born, and I felt the loss of never knowing them. Time-travel stories are a way of connecting to lost worlds—be they people, places, or events. They explore the Jewish mystical idea that the past, present, and future all exist at the same time but in separate dimensions. Once in a while, at least in stories, we get a chance to visit those alternate realities and gain an understanding we might not have otherwise.

~ About the Author ~

MALKA PENN is the author of a middle-grade novel, *The Hanukkah Ghosts,* and a picture book, *The Miracle of the Potato Latkes,* as well as numerous short stories and articles published in magazines. Besides writing and editing, she also curates art exhibits. She has two daughters and two grandchildren. Originally from Philadelphia, she lives in Connecticut with her husband.

Jerusalem Tunnel

~ Hanna Bandes Geshelin ~

Hunched in his sweatshirt, Dan slowed down, letting the tourists in front of him disappear beyond a turn. "It's my thirteenth birthday," he muttered, "and I'm stuck on this miserable archaeological tour in this cold, damp tunnel." He'd wanted to stay home and have a blowout Bar Mitzvah bash, like his friends. But his folks had brought him to Jerusalem. Now he was spending his birthday traipsing through a dim, narrow, boring tunnel beneath the city.

His folks were so excited about visiting the ancient sites that they had borrowed every book the library had on Israeli archaeology. Mom had even started a needlepoint of an ancient Israeli coin, which she worked every free moment. Neither cared that Dan wasn't interested in archaeology. Neither cared that he was missing the biggest basketball game of the season, or that without him his team didn't have a chance. It's my Bar Mitzvah, he thought, kicking a stone viciously. And I'm dragged around like a dog on a leash.

"Hurry up!" The stout man behind Dan poked his shoulder. Dan turned and glared. The man and his wife had been trying to pass Dan ever since the tour began, but the tunnel was narrow and both the man and his wife were very fat. Up ahead, Dan saw a little alcove. He stepped into it so that the couple could pass.

As Dan pressed his back against the uneven stones, a cold wind ruffled his jeans. Wind in a stone tunnel? Dan crouched to investigate. A large block of stone was set slightly back from the others, leaving a slot through which came a riffle of dank air. The wind also carried voices, and with a shock he realized they were his parents'. He heard his mother say, ". . . uncooperative." His father replied with ". . . selfish . . . lazy." Then he heard his own name. They were talking about him.

He jumped to his feet, his hands in such tight fists that his nails dug into his palms. Uncooperative, when you made me have my Bar Mitzvah here instead of at home with my buddies? Selfish, after you forced me to miss the big game? Lazy, because I wanted to skip this stupid tour?

Enraged, he kicked the wall. But instead of receiving a satisfying impact that would have jarred him back to reality, his foot continued forward. The rock slid out of the way as though it were greased. Dan was thrown off balance, stumbling toward the wall. He threw out his hands and caught himself, his head just inches from the stones.

The impact sent shock waves from the palms of his hands clear to his feet. He struggled to catch his breath. Then he felt something digging into his hand—something metal. It was a small coin, wedged between the stones. He wiggled it loose and studied it. On one side was a wine goblet with strange writing over it. On the other side, the writing encircled three pomegranates on a single stem. With a shock he realized that he was holding the model for his mom's needlepoint. How had it gotten into the crack? He rubbed the blackened coin. The mystery of the past rose about him, enveloping him in questions. Who had carried this coin? When was it used? How did it get stuck between two stones in the tunnel wall?

As he turned the coin over and over, he shivered. The draft was much stronger now. Crouching down, he studied the place he'd kicked. The rough stone had slid through the wall a foot or two. The dimly lit opening contrasted with the alcove where he stood, which was lit brightly by an electric light.

If I explore this secret tunnel, the light will guide me back, he thought. My Bar Mitzvah adventure. Maybe I'll find the lost Ark of the Covenant, like in that old Harrison Ford movie. It would make up for the rest of this miserable trip. He straightened, looking up and down the tourist tunnel. No one was in sight. He crouched down and scrambled through the opening.

The new tunnel was so low that he had to crawl. The cold wind blowing against his face chilled him, but a faint light drew him forward. The tunnel ended suddenly, leaving Dan in a spacious cavern. He stood up and dusted off his knees. Mist swirled. The slow, irregular drip-drip of water beat a counterpoint to his pounding heart. This is crazy, he thought. I should go back. He turned toward the tunnel. Its opening shone like a beacon. But something pulled him toward the darkness. He thrust his hands into his pockets and hunched his shoulders against the damp. His fingers wrapped around the coin. Heads I stay, tails I go.

The coin gleamed eerily in the dim light, three pomegranates on their stem. He rubbed the pomegranates, then tossed and caught the coin.

Suddenly he coughed. Smoke wafted through the hot, sunny plaza. A wail broke the stillness, and a crowd surged past, chased by two toga-clad soldiers with outstretched spears. Just as suddenly the plaza was empty.

I'm on stage, Dan thought. A play, like that *Julius Caesar* we saw in school last year. But all he could see was an alley to the left, another to the right, and between them, the plaza. His fingertips brushed the warm stones and rustled some dry weeds that had survived briefly in a crevice in the wall. A small, dusty brown lizard, the length of his finger, scurried across the stones, then squirmed between the wall and a wooden door, disappearing from view.

A door. For the first time Dan noticed that the plaza was lined with arches. Some were sealed with wooden doors and heavy locks, others were boarded and fastened shut. As he turned and stared at the plaza, he heard shouts and the sound of feet. More soldiers? I've got to get out of here! Dan looked for the opening through which he'd come, but it was gone. In its place was an arch with a partly open wooden door. Pushing the door wider, he stepped into a dark hallway, then shut the heavy wooden door behind him.

Saying a quick prayer of thanksgiving for the silent soles of his sneakers, he crept down the passage. After a few steps it opened into a small courtyard, where smoky sunlight filtered through the branches of a dying pomegranate tree. Across the courtyard was an open door. He started toward it, then stopped as a faint movement caught his eye. A rat? He took three steps toward some bushes. A branch moved, pushed aside by small, dirty fingers. A child.

Dan crouched down. "You can come out," he whispered. "I won't hurt you."

The bush rustled, and a small boy, perhaps seven years old, peeked out. "You're not a Roman soldier. Who are you?" demanded the boy.

"I'm Dan. I . . ." Dan stopped. "Is this a *play?*" He hoped it was. But he knew it wasn't.

"A play?" The child crept out from behind the bush, staring at Dan with a pitying look. "Did the Romans hit you on the head? Shabano was confused for three days after the Romans hit him."

"Who's Shabano?"

"He's . . . he was my brother." The child wiped his eyes with a dirty fist. "The Romans killed him, just like they killed Imma, Shifra, and Leah.

But they didn't kill me. I hid."

Dan wiped his sweating hands on his jeans and swallowed. Where was he? More important, *when* was he? And who were those icy-eyed soldiers? "W-w-w-why did the soldiers kill them?"

The child stamped his foot impatiently. "Because they want Jerusalem, silly! Because they want all the Jews dead. Because . . ." His face crumpled, and tears trickled down his thin cheeks. "Abba says they are angry because we don't want to be like them. They think they're so great, with their stone statues that they think are gods. They want us to bow to their stupid statues, their idols. Abba says we can't win. The Romans are too many and too well trained. And they like killing people. Jews hate to kill. So we get killed instead. Imma!" The child crossed his arms over his face and began sobbing. Dan drew the child to him, holding him as he sobbed.

Finally the child hiccuped and lifted his head. "Will you help me?"

Panic filled Dan. I want to go home! I don't know anything about this place. How can I help? But the child's huge, sad eyes begged Dan to stay. Dan swallowed hard. "Let's go look for your . . ." Dan stopped. Mother, he was about to say. But she was dead.

"Where's your father?"

The child hugged his skinny arms to his chest, rubbing his bare foot in the dust. He sniffed and looked at Dan, his eyes dark pools in his thin face. "He was at the Temple. He worked there."

Past tense, thought Dan. "He's dead too?"

The child nodded. "Shabano said the Romans killed everyone at the Temple early this morning. Now they are destroying the Temple. He said that's what is burning. And when the earth shakes, it's not an earthquake. It's the wall of the Temple, falling."

As if echoing the boy, a huge, dull crash resounded in the distance, and the earth trembled.

The Temple. Dan stepped backward. Yesterday, when touring the southern part of the Temple wall, the guide had pointed out huge, toppled stones. Some still showed the black, charred proof of the boy's words. But that was almost two thousand years ago, on the Ninth of Av in the year 70 C.E. The Romans had pushed burning logs between the huge stones of the Temple. The fire had caused moisture trapped in the stones to expand, breaking the rocks apart and toppling the walls.

Yesterday, that tragedy had seemed remote. Irrelevant to Dan's life.

Part of the far distant past. Today it was . . . today.

Dan tightened his grip on the child.

"What's your name?"

"Everyone calls me Dudy," the child whispered. "But my name's Daniel. Daniel ben-Matityahu ha-Levi."

Icy fingers clutched Dan's chest. "But that's *my* name!" Did I fall and hit my head? he wondered. Is this a dream? But the boy's scrawny arm felt real beneath his fingers.

The boy stared back at Dan, his eyes huge. "*Your* name?"

"I'm . . . I'm also Daniel ben-Matityahu ha-Levi." A huge knot rose in his throat. He swallowed hard, then coughed in the smoky air. "Everyone calls me Dan."

Dudy bit his lower lip. He looked Dan up and down. Dan felt as though the child were looking into every corner of his heart. Finally the child spoke. "I never knew anyone with my name before. It's a sign that you've come to help me."

"How . . . how can I help?"

"Help me send off Shabano's pigeons."

"*Pigeons?*" Soldiers everywhere, and he's worried about birds?

"We have to let people know what's happening!" Dudy pulled on Dan's arm. "I can't do it alone."

"I don't know what you're talking about." Dan jumped to his feet. "I've got to get out of here. This is crazy."

"Please! If you don't help me, who will?"

"But what do pigeons have to do with messages? Use . . . " His voice trailed off. He was going to say e-mail, or phone. But that was crazy, it was the year 70. Oh God, what I am doing here?

Dudy tugged at Dan's arm.

"The pigeons will carry our notes to our friends in Hebron and Beth-Horon and Aphek and other cities. I can't reach the ink and parchment, but you could. You're taller than Shabano. And I can't tie the messages to the pigeons, Shabano does . . . did that. My knots always come open. *You* can tie the knots."

Dan wasn't so sure, but the child was desperate. He dragged Dan into the house. "Don't look," he whispered as he threaded his way between the bodies of his mother, brother, and sisters. The stench of death filled Dan's nostrils. A sour taste filled his mouth and he swallowed hard, trying not to throw up.

"Hurry. We have to release the pigeons soon so they can leave the city before dark. They roost at nightfall." Dudy pulled him into another room. "There are the writing things." He pointed to the wall. High up, almost above Dan's head, was a niche. In it were several scrolls, a pile of thin parchment, a ceramic bottle with a stopper, and a cup holding several large feathers. Dan glanced around. Except for a stone table pushed against the wall, the room was bare.

"Don't you have stools? Chairs? Rugs?"

"We burned them long ago, for cooking. When we still had food."

With a shock, Dan realized that Dudy wasn't just a skinny kid. He was starved, like the skeletal children of the Holocaust. When yesterday's guide said that the Romans had besieged Jerusalem, causing terrible starvation, the words had meant nothing to Dan. But starvation clearly meant something to Dudy.

I usually have a snack in my pockets, thought Dan. He felt around. His fingers closed on a stick of gum. Nope, no food value. In his back pocket he found a handful of dried apricots wrapped in a paper napkin. He'd taken them from the breakfast buffet at the hotel, in case he got hungry, then forgotten them. He almost passed the packet over to Dudy. Then he remembered a Holocaust survivor who had spoken at his religious school. She'd said that some Holocaust survivors had died the day they were liberated from the camps because they ate too much, too fast.

"Here, Dudy." He held out one of the apricots.

The child's eyes opened wide. He reached out a dirty hand, then pulled back. "It's yours," he whispered.

"I don't need it. Please."

The fingers darted out and closed over the apricot as though Dudy were afraid Dan would change his mind. He brought the fruit up to his open mouth, then stopped. He stretched out his hand, holding the dried fruit up in the air, and shouted a blessing. Only then did he jam the apricot into his mouth and start to chew.

"Eat it slowly!"

Dudy nodded, his jaw working a mile a minute. While he chewed, Dan took down the writing supplies and set them on the stone table. He took a quill from the cup and studied it. "I don't know how to write with this. And I can hardly write Hebrew."

Dudy swallowed the last bit of apricot, then wiped his mouth on his arm. "Thank you, that was—what did you say?"

"I can hardly write Hebrew. And I don't know how to write with this." He waved the quill.

Dudy stamped his foot. "I thought you were my friend. You gave me an apricot. Now you don't want to be my friend. So go away. If you won't help, leave me alone!"

"No, Dudy, please!" Dan reached for the child, but Dudy ducked out of his grasp and ran back into the first room. He crouched down beside the body of his mother, tucked his head down, and began to rock back and forth, wailing.

Dan knelt down beside the small child. "Dudy, you have a job. You have to teach me what to do. I'm a stranger here. A . . . a messenger."

Dudy froze. He sniffed hard. Then he turned and gazed at Dan. "A messenger? Like an angel? Is that why you look so strange?"

"I . . ." Dan hesitated. "I'm a messenger from the future. From a long time away in the future."

Dudy sat back on his heels and stared. "Are you a Jew?"

"Yes."

"There are Jews in the future?"

"Yes."

Dudy ran his fingers over Dan's arm. He pinched Dan's sweatshirt, then cautiously touched the sparkly lettering on the front. "You're real. You're a Jew. And you're from the future."

Dudy's thin fingers pressed into Dan's arm as he pulled himself up. "Abba said the Romans will kill all the Jews."

"They won't. They'll kill lots, but they'll take others to Rome as slaves. Remember when the Jews were slaves in Egypt, and then they were freed? The Jews who go to Rome as slaves will be free one day, too."

Dudy stared at the ground for a long moment. He sighed and wiped his tear-streaked face with his sleeve. "So God sent you to help. Come." He clutched Dan's hand and pulled him back to the inner room. He showed Dan how to dip the quill in the ink, write a few letters until the ink was used, then dip again.

While Dan practiced writing with the quill, Dudy worked on the note. He whispered the words, his tongue licking his upper lip in concentration. In a few moments he smoothed out the note and read it aloud. "9 Av. The

Romans have killed many people. They are making the rest slaves. The Temple wall is falling. The city is burning. Daniel ben-Matityahu ha-Levi."

He put his note on the table. A faint smile crossed his face as he studied Dan's writing. "Your writing is as slow and as bad as mine. We need nine more copies. We'll both write."

Dan looked at Dudy's note. "I'll try." I sure wish I'd studied harder, he added to himself. The two boys bent over their quills. For a long time the room was silent except for the *scritch-scritch* of feather on parchment.

"That's all." Dudy set his quill in the cup and looked at Dan. "Let's go." He clutched the parchments in one hand. With his other hand he reached for Dan. "The pigeons are on the roof."

He led Dan past the bodies into the courtyard. Steps to the roof were built into the courtyard wall. "Keep low so the Romans don't see you," Dudy whispered as they climbed to the rooftop.

The smoke was much worse on the roof. To the east, flames danced against a smoke-red sky. Shrieks and the tread of soldiers filled the air. Panic raced through Dan. In spite of the heat, cold fear gripped his chest. I'll never get home, he thought. Then he glanced at Dudy. The small boy's face was flushed, his dark eyes burning like candles. "As the soldiers killed Shabano, he yelled, 'The pigeons, the pigeons!' He was telling me that I had to send the message since he couldn't. Now I'm sending it, as he asked. I can die in peace." He seemed to grow, as though in fulfilling his mission he was becoming a man.

"You . . . you won't die," whispered Dan. The words caught in his throat. He wanted to ask, "Where do you get your courage?" But he knew that Dudy wouldn't understand the question. He was just doing what he had to do. As I am, Dan realized. Holding on to that thought, he fought down his panic.

Then they were at the dovecote. The pigeons fluttered when they saw Dudy. One flew from its open cage, landing on Dudy's head. Dudy reached up to stroke the bird. "When we ran out of food, we opened the cages. They go out to eat, but they come back. They know this is home," he said. He opened a metal box, removing fine thread and a small knife. "We roll the message around a leg and tie it," he explained. "I'll hold the birds. You tie."

When each bird was ready, Dudy opened his hands and gave a little toss. The pigeon fluttered, then flew away.

Finally Dudy reached up and lifted down the pigeon that stood on his head. "This is mine." He kissed the sleek bird's head. "He'll fly to my uncle in

Hebron." As he stroked the bird, a feather loosened itself from its wing. Dudy tucked the feather in his belt. When the note was tied securely, Dudy kissed the bird again. Then he raised him high in the air and released him. The bird circled once, then sped toward freedom.

Dudy and Dan watched the bird disappear. Occasionally the younger boy's shoulders shook, but he was silent. Finally he turned around. "Now we can die, too," he whispered, taking Dan's hand.

"The Romans will take many Jews as slaves. They will live."

"I don't want to be a slave by myself."

"You have to go if you have a chance. The Jewish people need to live. *You* need to live."

"Will you come with me?"

"I can't," Dan said. "I have to find my way back to my own time." Please, God, get me home, he prayed silently. He reached into his pocket and pulled out the napkin-wrapped packet. "Take the rest of my apricots. Eat them slowly, so you don't get sick." He waited while Dudy tucked the packet into his robe. Then he bent down and hugged the boy. "I promise, you'll live to have a son. He'll be Matityahu ben-Daniel ha-Levi. His son or grandson will be Daniel ben-Matityahu ha-Levi, and so on until I'm born." He stood up, drawing Dudy upright. "Do you understand? There will be many generations of Jews, fathers and sons, one after another, from you to me."

Dudy nodded.

The sound of marching soldiers mingled with the sound of shuffling feet. Soon the two boys spied the helmeted heads of soldiers leading a crowd of Jews. More soldiers marched behind.

"Come," said Dudy to Dan. "I'm ready. We cannot hide here forever." He pulled Dan down the last steps into the courtyard. Dan waited while Dudy went into the room where the bodies of his family lay. Then the boy came back out. He clutched Dan's waist and stared into his eyes. "You said before that the Jews will be free. That's the truth? We won't be slaves forever?"

"Yes, truly, the Jews will be free. It will be a long time, but we will."

Dudy nodded. "Then I'll go. I'll stay alive for my family. And for you, Daniel ben-Matityahu ha-Levi-from-the-future. Come."

Dudy pulled him through the hallway to the plaza. A moment later the Romans rounded the corner. A stocky soldier poked at Dudy with the flat of his sword. "Get moving."

Dudy tugged at Dan's hand. "Come, Dan," he whispered.

"Move on, dog!" The soldier raised his sword at Dudy, ignoring Dan.

"Go, Dudy. He doesn't see me," said Dan.

Dudy released Dan's hand. He pulled the pigeon feather out of his robe and handed it to Dan. Then he ducked past the soldier into the crowd. "Good-bye, angel," Dudy called. "Good-bye."

Dan watched until Dudy was out of sight. Now he could feel the fire approach. As he dropped the feather into his pocket, he felt the small silver coin. He rubbed the pomegranates once, twice, three times.

The sky darkened, and sounds quieted. A damp chill replaced the hot, smoky air. Now the only light was a small square of dimness. Dan turned and crawled through the opening, toward the light that glimmered far ahead.

As he approached the tourist tunnel, Dan could hear people coming, footsteps and the welcome sounds of English. Through the opening he watched a parade of Nikes, Reeboks, and Teva sandals. Shoes from his own age. A huge weight lifted from him.

When the last pair of feet had passed, Dan scrambled into the tourist tunnel. Reaching into his pocket, he pulled out the coin. He held it by the rim, careful not to rub it. Spotting the small crevice from which he'd taken the coin, he jammed it back. "There," he thought. "Now it's safe." Then he studied the irregular surface of the stone that had opened into the tunnel, looking for a way to pull it forward. Grooves ran a few inches back from the front edge along both sides of the block. Using these hand-holds, he tugged at the stone. As though greased, it slid easily into place, sending him back onto his heels. He pressed his hand to his chest, catching his breath. Then he eyed the wall. The stones looked as though they'd never been disturbed. He shook his head, then stood up. He straightened and stretched. Somehow, he felt bigger. Older, or maybe wiser than he'd been before his adventure had started. He reached into his pocket again, closing his fingers around Dudy's gift. He pulled out the soft, gray feather and stroked it across his cheek. Then he tucked it back into his pocket and sprinted after the retreating tourists.

~ Background Note from the Author ~

When I toured the excavations in Jerusalem in 1998, I kept thinking about the children and grown-ups who lived during the terrible days when the Temple was destroyed. Many of them were taken as slaves to Rome, where they managed to survive and to keep their faith and traditions alive. Some must have been my ancestors. In Jerusalem, I also saw lots of bored American kids—also descendants of those slaves—whose parents were dragging them from site to site. I thought, "If those kids could just imagine what their ancestors' lives were really like, they wouldn't be bored." This story is my small attempt to help kids feel that the Jewish past was once very much alive.

Thanks to the staff at Archaeological Seminars of Jerusalem for their fabulous tours of Jerusalem's archaeological sites and their help with historical information for this story.

~ About the Author ~

HANNA BANDES GESHELIN wrote technical manuals and nonfiction articles for many years but only began writing stories after she became a professional storyteller. She has done many kinds of work and lived in many places, including Israel. Now she lives in Worcester, Massachusetts, with her husband, where her present jobs include working in a library, helping her husband run an apartment complex, and writing. She toured the Jerusalem tunnel and the southern Temple wall on a hot August day in 1998, exactly 1928 years and 18 days after the destruction of the Second Temple.

Hanukkah Light

~ Janni Lee Simner ~

The boy appeared in the flames on the first night of Hanukkah. Zack sat gloomily alone in the kitchen, staring into the menorah's single candle—not counting the *shammash* candle, which existed only to light the others anyway. In the living room, Mom laughed with Paul and his kids, Samantha and Kaitlyn, as she helped them decorate the Christmas tree. You'd think they could have chosen some other night.

As Zack watched, the candle's small flame seemed to grow, filling his sight, turning the kitchen to shadows at its edges. Zack should have been frightened, but he just watched, fascinated. A window opened within the flame, onto a world of bright blowing sand. Zack squinted at the hot desert light. A boy stood braced against the wind, squinting back. His clothes were gray tatters. His long black hair was tangled about his face, framing dark eyes, high cheekbones, a long nose. In one hand he held a tarnished dagger. He shifted the dagger's weight from hand to hand, then jabbed at the air. A look of fierce pride crossed his face. He gripped the dagger tighter.

"Zack, why don't you join us—" Zack started at his mother's voice. So did the boy; his eyes darted warily back and forth. For a moment his gaze met Zack's, and Zack knew they saw each other perfectly.

"Oh Zack, you should have waited!" The flame flickered, became only candlelight once more. Mom burst into the room. "I was planning to light candles soon—" She left and returned, her arms full of gifts. Kait followed at her heels, shrieking, "Presents! Presents!" Zack sighed.

"Here, let me help." Paul took the wrapped packages from Mom's arms and set them on the table. Sam stood in the doorway, looking bored.

"I'm sorry Zack," Mom said. "It's just that there's so much to juggle, with the new house, and the tree—"

"It's all right," Zack lied. He hated the house, he hated the tree, and he hated Mom's marrying Paul in the first place. Every time he told her, though, they got into a huge fight.

Zack watched the candle burn down to a stub, thinking about the boy instead. He wondered if the kid had been real, or if he'd just imagined him.

~

The next night Zack saw him again.

Mom wasn't late that night. As soon as the sun set, she and Zack lit the candles and said the prayers together. Mom put an arm around Zack's shoulders while they spoke, and for a few moments it almost felt like old times, except that Dad was off living in California rather than lighting candles with them.

Instead of Dad, Paul and his kids stood around the table, looking uncomfortable. Sam and Kait kept exchanging long looks. Paul smiled, as if he were trying to be polite but really wished he wasn't there.

"What's with the funny words?" Sam finally asked.

"Sam!" Paul said. "Show some respect."

"It's Hebrew," Zack told her, wishing she would just disappear.

"You have a problem with English?" Sam pressed.

Zack didn't answer. Of all the things he hated about the new house, he hated Sam most. She was in middle school, just a couple of years older than him. Kait was younger, in kindergarten. Maybe that was why she wasn't as annoying.

"What do the words mean?" Paul asked, more tactfully.

"They're just a way of thanking God for helping us celebrate this holiday of lights," Mom said with a smile. She'd never smiled much around Dad.

"Are we done yet?" Sam asked.

"Sam—" Paul warned.

"May I please go now?" Sam tried instead. Paul nodded, and Sam left them. Zack heard her fiddling with the living-room stereo. The others soon followed. Zack started to leave, but as he did the flames of the candles—two of them now—grew once more. He whirled and saw the boy and the desert in their light.

One of the boy's cheeks had been cut; blood trickled down his face. He clutched the hilt of the dagger, which he wore in a belt the same gray as his other rags.

"Who are you?" Zack whispered, Sam and his mother both forgotten.

The boy looked up, startled. His face settled into a frown. "Who are *you?*"

Before Zack could answer, he turned and strode away, disappearing into the desert dust. Zack shivered. He knew he hadn't imagined anything this time.

In the living room, Sam put a CD in the player. As Zack entered the room, he heard, *Silent night, holy night . . .*

Sam turned the volume up when she saw him.

"Cut it out," Zack snapped.

"Cut what out?" Sam grabbed the remote and sprawled out on the couch, setting the volume louder still.

"Turn it down!" Paul called from his office down the hall.

"But it's Christmas music!" Sam shouted back.

"I don't care!" Paul yelled.

Sam sighed and lowered the music a fraction.

Mom entered the room. "I think it sounds nice." She raised her voice to be heard. "Nothing wrong with a little Christmas spirit."

Zack scowled. Mom had been saying stuff like that for weeks. Have a little Christmas spirit, for Paul and the girls' sake. There's no harm in it. It's just part of being a family.

It had never been part of their family before.

Zack looked to the corner of the room where the tree stood. It was completely decorated now, with strings of popcorn, silver tinsel, and colored glass balls. A lopsided silver angel brushed the ceiling. "Beautiful," Paul had announced the night before.

But Zack thought the tree was awful. Christmas trees and Christmas music were fine in other people's houses. In his house, they felt like alien invaders that wouldn't go away.

~

"My name is Zachariah," the boy said on the third night.

"Mine too," Zack told him. Somehow having a name made the boy seem less creepy—and more real. Behind Zachariah the desert rolled in hills of sand. Farther away, smoke rose from a fire.

In the living room, Zack's mom and stepfamily arranged a nativity scene above the fireplace.

Kait burst into the kitchen. "Your mom said to ask if you want to help."

All at once, boy and desert were gone. Zack turned irritably to Kait. "I'm Jewish, remember?"

Kait looked up at him. "But this is Christmas," she said, puzzled.

"I don't celebrate Christmas."

"*Everyone* celebrates Christmas."

Zack turned back to the candles, but no matter how long he stared, Zachariah did not return.

~

The fourth night Zachariah seemed to expect Zack. He stared at him through the flames, growing sharper and more real with each candle. The others didn't seem to notice. From across the table, Sam hummed "Rudolph the Red-Nosed Reindeer" under her breath. Zack wished he had a remote control to turn *her* off.

As soon as everyone else left, the boy spoke, in a hard, fierce voice too old for a kid. "I am Zachariah, the son of Jorub, who is the son of Saul. But I serve Judah Maccabee, because my parents have turned to the false Syrian gods set before them by King Antiochus—God curse his name!"

"Maccabee?" Zack squeaked. He went to Hebrew school; he knew the story. The Syrian Greeks had captured a Jewish temple, put up statues of their gods, and refused to let the Jews worship. After a long battle the Maccabees freed the temple and the Jews returned. Only a day's supply of holy oil remained to purify the place so they could worship again, but somehow the oil burned for eight days, until the Jews could make more. A miracle—and the reason for lighting Hanukkah candles.

Somehow Zack was seeing back in time, all the way back to the Maccabees. He shivered again, not unpleasantly this time, and looked at the boy with new respect.

"Who are *you?*" Zachariah demanded. "What gods do you worship?" By some magic—perhaps the same magic that let Zack see him—he spoke English. Zack hadn't thought about that before, because he hadn't known who the boy was.

"I—I'm Zack. Zack Cohen."

Zachariah scowled. "You don't look Jewish. Let alone like a Kohain, a member of the priestly class."

"Hey! You can't tell who's Jewish just by looking at them."

To Zack's surprise, the boy's face softened. "This is true. My father and his father look as Jewish as I, for all that they've accepted Antiochus's evil ways." He tugged at his ragged shirt. The sleeves were too short, and his bony wrists poked out the ends. "You don't mention your parents. Have they, too, taken to foreign ways?"

Mom entered the kitchen. Startled, Zack turned around and watched her rummage through the fridge. She pulled out flour, butter, sugar, and eggs, as well as a large mixing bowl. Mom hadn't baked since before she and Dad had begun fighting.

"Christmas cookies!" Kait screeched, joining Mom with her arms full of cookie cutters.

Zack's stomach sank. He'd hoped she was baking for him. "Yeah," he whispered to Zachariah. "Yeah, they have."

"I am sorry," Zachariah said from behind him.

But when Zack looked back at the candles, the boy was gone.

~

On the fifth night Paul had to stay late at work. He said he was sorry that he couldn't light candles with them, but not as if he meant it. Sam declared that if her dad didn't have to be there, neither did she. Kait said she didn't want to be the only one, so Zack and Mom lit candles alone. Zack watched his mother, wondering if maybe she didn't want to be there, either.

As soon as Mom left the kitchen, Zachariah appeared, holding his dagger triumphantly. Rather than empty desert, a stone tower rose behind him. "We've reclaimed the Temple!" the boy cried. "We've smashed their pagan idols and returned our holy objects to their places!"

"Cool!" Zack still couldn't believe he was watching part of that story. For a moment, what Mom or Paul wanted didn't matter.

The boy grinned. "Tomorrow we fight for the holy city as well!"

Zack blinked at that. He'd thought the story ended when the Maccabees got the temple back. But the boy pounded a fist at the air and ran toward the towers.

"Ready to go shopping?" Mom asked, returning to the room.

"Shopping? Shopping for what?"

"Gifts, of course. With Paul out of the house, this is the perfect time."

"We already went shopping for gifts." Zack had even bought presents for Paul, Sam, and Kait, which he thought was more than fair.

"Not Hanukkah gifts. Christmas gifts. Christmas is only a week away."

"I don't want any Christmas gifts."

Mom sighed. "Sometimes being a family is about compromise, you know."

Zack scowled. "I don't see *her* compromising." He gestured to the living room, where Sam lay on the couch, wearing headphones turned up loud enough for him to hear "Santa Claus Is Coming to Town."

"That's between Sam and Paul. I'm talking about you."

"I don't want any Christmas gifts," Zack repeated. He tried to stay calm, but anger edged his words.

Mom sighed again and shook her head. "You could at least try, Zack."

But she didn't complain about Sam not trying. Instead she invited Sam and Kait both along. The three of them left the house together, talking and laughing. Zack watched them go. The anger grew hotter, until he thought he'd explode. "She's *my* mom," he yelled. The empty room didn't answer. "It's my house!"

He stormed into the living room and kicked the Christmas tree. A glass ball tumbled to the floor and shattered. Zack grabbed another ball and threw it down himself. Then another, and another. It felt good to hear the glass break. It felt good to finally do something, instead of watching and complaining and having no one understand. He thought of Zachariah, smashing the pagan idols, and threw harder. When he ran out of ornaments he tore down the popcorn strands, the tinsel. He shook the tree until the stupid angel fell down, too.

"Zack?"

Zack stopped, surprised by the quiet voice. Paul watched him, his face unreadable.

Zack's stomach clenched. Suddenly he didn't feel so good after all. He felt sick. Without a word, he fled to his room.

~

On the sixth night of Hanukkah, Zack didn't light candles, because except for school he was grounded to his room.

When she'd seen the broken ornaments, Mom had yelled and screamed. Paul had stared at the tree, looking sad. Kait had burst into tears. Sam had cursed him out, using words she wasn't supposed to know.

Now Zack lay on his bed, glumly playing a video game. Sam kicked his door, hard. "I hate you, Zack Cohen! I hate everything about you! I wish my dad had never been stupid enough to marry your mom!" Zack stared at his game, pretending he didn't care. But he felt awful. His stomach twisted into queasy knots.

Maybe Zachariah would understand. But Zachariah wasn't there.

~

On the seventh night, Zack came home from school and found his room trashed.

Clothes lay everywhere. Notebooks, too, their pages ripped out. Even the sheets had been torn from his bed. And pieces of broken glass Christmas ornaments were scattered like confetti over it all.

Fury burned the sick feeling away. Zack stormed across the hall and threw Sam's door open. "How dare you!" he cried. She was the only one who got home before he did, because middle school let out earlier. "How dare you?"

"Don't you know how to knock?" Sam stared innocently at the ceiling. Zack wanted to hit her.

"You just wait! I'll get you back!" He didn't care if he was grounded for life; he'd make Sam pay. He stomped back to his own room, slamming his door shut behind him.

"I'll get you back twice as bad!" Sam called down the hall. "You know I will!"

Zack stared furiously at his room. He picked up a handful of colored glass and tossed it into the trash. A shard sliced his palm, and it bled. Zack cursed under his breath.

Just wait until Sam left her room. Zack would get even then.

When Mom got home Zack said nothing. She'd only lecture him about compromising again, and that was the last thing he wanted to do now.

Mom was still mad at him, anyway; she barely spoke as they lit candles together. No one else joined them. Paul had gone out shopping instead.

Zachariah appeared as soon as Zack used the *shammash* to light the first candle. His face, hands, and clothes were all splattered with blood. Zack stumbled back, dropping the *shammash* as he did. It hit the floor and flickered out, but the Maccabee boy remained, clutching his dagger grimly. Smoke surrounded him; Zack couldn't tell where he stood.

"Zack, what's wrong with you?" With a disgusted sigh, Mom picked up the *shammash* and relit it, then lit the remaining candles. Within their flames, Zachariah grew larger and larger, until he stood much taller than Zack.

"What happened?" Zack whispered. Horror made his hands shake.

"What happened to what?" Mom asked.

"We pursued them!" A smile lit Zachariah's bloodstained features. "We pursued, and God was on our side! We killed many Syrians and drove them from our lands! But then they turned on us, and many of our men died as well. But tomorrow we attack anew! Even now, the Maccabee brothers make their plans!"

"But when does it end?" The story was supposed to end at the Temple.

"End?" Zachariah asked, as if he didn't understand the word.

"Zack, are you okay?" Mom asked.

Zack looked down at his hands. A thin, red line was all that remained where he'd cut himself on the glass. It doesn't end, he thought, wondering what Sam would do after he got even, and what he would do after that. His throat felt dry; he couldn't speak.

He looked back to the flames. Zachariah stared into the distance, at something Zack couldn't see. The boy absently rubbed the dried blood from his forehead and kept staring.

A car pulled into the driveway. Zack turned as Paul stepped into the house, a shopping bag in one hand. Through the plastic, Zack saw a box of Christmas ornaments.

He thought of shattered glass. He thought of the blood on Zachariah's face. It had to end somewhere. He had to make it end. He looked at the bag of ornaments Paul held, and he took a shaky step toward his stepfather.

"Zack—" Mom warned. Paul watched him warily.

Zack swallowed. For a moment he wasn't sure he could speak. "You want any help with that?" he asked at last.

Paul hesitated, then gave Zack a long, considering look. "All right," he said. "Why don't you give me a hand?"

It took a long time to decorate the tree, just the two of them, not speaking. As Zack worked, the anger in him burned down a little.

"It's nice to finally see some family spirit here!" Mom said as she walked through the room once.

But that wasn't the point. That wasn't the point at all.

~

On the eighth night, many things remained the same.

Zack still didn't like the tree. He still wanted to get rid of it, but instead he just left it alone.

Sam still hated him. "About time you did something useful," she'd said, scowling when she saw Zack helping Paul decorate. But when Zack had returned to his room that night, his clothes had been folded up, and the broken glass was gone.

On the eighth night Kait wanted to sing Christmas carols. Mom asked Zack to join them. Zack refused. "I'll just listen," he said. Mom started to protest, but Paul stopped her. "No sense making someone sing against their will." He laughed, but his eyes, as they met Zack's, were quite serious.

Later, as Mom and Zack set eight candles in the menorah, Paul watched solemnly. "Want to help?" Zack asked, offering him a candle.

"I'll just watch." Paul didn't seem nearly as uncomfortable as before.

Mom sighed. Mom still didn't understand that being a family didn't always mean acting alike—or believing alike. It meant giving each person the space to be who they were.

Zack lit the first candle. Through the flame, Zachariah stared back at him, while sand blew all around. Zachariah's ragged clothes were clean now, but the dagger still hung from his belt. "Never give up," he whispered fiercely, clutching the hilt.

"I haven't," Zack said.

"Never stop fighting," the boy went on.

"That's not the same."

Zachariah didn't have the space to believe how he wanted. Maybe he had no choice but to fight. Maybe he did—Zack didn't know. All he knew was that here and now, he did have a choice.

Zack lit the rest of the candles. He and Mom recited the Hebrew prayer together, while Paul watched in respectful silence. From the doorway, Sam and Kait watched, too.

Zack stayed in the kitchen a long time after they left, but he did not look into the flames again.

~ Background Note from the Author ~

For years I've wondered what ghosts we might see if we looked deeply enough into the Hanukkah flames. The holiday has its roots in a grim war story, one that ended not with the successful rededication of the Temple, but years later, with the Maccabee brothers dead and the knowledge that there were battles yet to be fought and walls yet to be built. How does this troubling tale relate to the joyous winter festival we now celebrate? I wasn't sure—so I wrote "Hanukkah Light" to find out.

~ About the Author ~

JANNI LEE SIMNER is the author of the best-selling Phantom Rider trilogy (*Ghost Horse, The Haunted Trail,* and *Ghost Vision*), published by Scholastic. She's also published more than two dozen short stories in anthologies and magazines such as *Girls' Life, A Starfarer's Dozen, Bruce Coville's Book of Magic,* and *A Glory of Unicorns.* She was born in New York but made her way west as soon as she could, and currently lives in Tucson, Arizona.

My Grandma's Ghost

~ Carol Snyder ~

A re we there yet?" I asked for the millionth time.

"Not yet," said my younger sister, Jaimie. Every year on Passover, my family and I go to a *seder* at my grandfather's house. Since he re-married after my grandma died three years ago, I don't just have a step-grandmother. I have stepaunts and stepuncles and stepcousins—an entire staircase of new family.

There are always two tables with place cards carefully arranged on each, usually with names misspelled. When my grandma was alive, there was only one table and we sat wherever we wanted to. I always sat next to Grandma and Grandpa. Now I'm always placed at the children's table. Some day I'm going to make it to the adult table, where I can at least get to talk to my grandfather. Since the steps, I don't get to see him that often, and never alone like the old times. Maybe this will be the year.

When I was little, Grandpa and I would play with matchbox cars on the floor, on a piece of plywood he made into roads and villages by drawing on it. He's seventy-five now, and I don't expect him to get down on the floor. It would be too hard for him to get up. But it would be nice to have a conversation where he asks me about school and where I can mention memories of Grandma and us and keep her memory alive without hurting anyone's feelings, like my stepgrandmother's.

"I sure do miss Grandma," I said, as we drove.

"I know you do," Mom answered. "We all do."

We were trying to survive the great exodus from suburban New Jersey to Jericho, Long Island, which involved the L.I.E.—the Long Island Express-way—which is a lie because if it were an expressway, the cars would move and not just sit there like the longest parking lot in the world, as the traffic helicopter people call it. I think the Jewish Exodus from Egypt was faster.

I can't read in the car because it makes me nauseous. I can't listen to my loud music because it makes my father nauseous, and my Walkman walked.

You give Jaimie a tissue with a rubber band around a stuffed part that makes the tissue look like a ghost, and she can amuse herself for hours making up *Casper, the Friendly Ghost* TV shows. The most creative thing I can do is take two of my own fingers and turn them into ice-skaters or dancers and run contests and shows. But it's hard to be creative when you're starving. I mean hunger that rivals fasting on Yom Kippur, which I don't mind because it's a challenge and helps me realize what starving people and the homeless must face every day. What I don't understand is why people are invited to a *seder* at sundown, around six P.M., and don't get a thing to eat until eight P.M. except for some parsley dipped in salt water, which tastes delicious by then.

I looked at Jaimie's tissue ghost, and that's when I missed Grandma even more. I tried to remember the smell of her perfume.

Grandma and I always had this special thing with each other. I could just think about her and the phone would ring and I'd pick up the receiver and hear her voice. Then other times I would have to call her, not just want to but have to, and she'd answer and say, "Ariel, I was just thinking of you." Then I'd laugh and she'd say, "This is getting spooky."

"I wish Grandma could come back to help me out now and then when I miss her or need her," I said out loud. I remember at her funeral the rabbi said, "The soul has a separate existence of its own, and the grave is only a stopping-off station on the long road to eternity."

Maybe Grandma's soul has reached eternity, and maybe she can be wherever she is called to. I wished that somehow, tonight, Grandma's soul, or ghost, whatever, could figure out a way to get me seated near Grandpa at the adult table.

"We're there!" Jaimie said as we rounded the corner.

"Finally," I said, then added, "When can we go home? I miss my real Grandma. I don't want a replacement one."

"Calm down, Ariel," my mother said.

"Give your stepgrandmother and her family a chance," my father added.

"Remember how she passed the oatmeal test?" Jaimie reminded me. We'd made her stir and stir till the oatmeal was as smooth and creamy as

Grandma always made it for us.

"You're younger," I said. "I knew Grandma longer. That's why I miss her more."

It's not that my stepgrandmother isn't nice. She is. She never forgets a birthday or special occasion, and she picks out presents I really like. She makes Grandpa very happy, and my mom says she takes good care of him and keeps him healthy. She doesn't let him eat three portions of everything or drive when he's sleepy. They take trips to foreign countries on a big ship, and she brings back presents for all the steps and us.

The driveway was filled with cars and should probably have had a sign saying *Lot full.* We parked on the street, and Jaimie and I burst out of the car, glad to be free. My grandfather was waving to us from the open doorway. I got a sad feeling because arriving used to be my favorite part when my grandma was next to him. Now my stepgrandma gave a quick wave and went off with one of the steps.

We went inside, and after several octopus hugs I slowly made my way to the adults' table to check the seating cards. The table looked beautiful with the silver cup waiting to be filled with wine for the spirit of Elijah. Seeing the embroidered matzah cover that I remember my Grandma making when I was seven and she was teaching me to cross-stitch was like an ache in me, making me miss her from deep inside and wish that her spirit could come to me.

I touched the stitching. I found Grandpa's place card and walked around the table without finding my name. This could mean only one thing. I was eleven years old, but I would still be at the children's table. It was hopeless. I'd probably not even get to say a full sentence to Grandpa.

"Grandma," I prayed again inside my head, "I need some help with this." But nothing happened. I don't know how far away a person's spirit is, so maybe, I thought, it takes more time than a phone call to find my grandma's ghost.

I walked to the children's table, which did not have fine crystal glasses or my grandma's embroidered matzah cover. It had a paper towel decorated in sloppy blue Jewish stars made by one of the steps in nursery school and a paper *seder* plate with a shank bone, roasted egg, and bitter herbs all ready.

The doorbell kept ringing in the background, and I could picture the bed in the guest room getting piled high with coats and jackets. I wished I could be hidden underneath them instead of finding my place card at the worst seat in the house; not even near my sister, Jaimie, but squished between Evan the Obnoxious and Gregory the Gregarious, stepcousins who would step all over me. I had learned that word, gregarious, years ago in a spelling bee I was in.

Gregory was already talking, yak, yak, yak. "I'm hungry. I'm starving. Can't a kid get something to eat around here?" he said, and started kicking the table leg.

"It's Passover," I said, sitting next to him, "Remember, we don't eat for a while. And could you stop kicking." I wanted to stick an apple in his mouth to shut him up.

Evan squeezed in next to me and reached over to tickle me.

"You could just say hello, you know, and could you take your elbows off the table?" I said.

Jaimie and I exchanged looks, and Evan reached across to tickle her.

"Grandma," I called out in my mind, again, "This is getting ridiculous." I thought I saw a flutter of Grandma's embroidered matzah cover at the adult table, but I probably just imagined it.

I took a deep breath. When my grandmother used to make a *seder*, I could smell the chicken soup and matzah balls and pot roast and *tsimmes* as if the air were heavy with good aromas. Now I smelled only perfume, and it wasn't the one I was used to. A sad feeling filled my heart as my stepgrandmother patted my head as she walked by.

Two younger steps weren't seated yet. I glanced over at the black-painted baby grand piano that used to be polished mahogany wood. It was my grandma's treasure. I remembered how she taught me to play "Hot Cross Buns" on it ever so gently. Now the steps were ganging up and banging on it, and not even Grandpa was stopping them. Grandma never would have allowed it.

"Grandma," I called, but her spirit probably couldn't even hear me above the noise of everyone talking at once.

Grandpa gave out the haggadahs, which by now were typed pages with stains of past *seders* on them. I think that as he gets older he takes out pages here and there to get to the parsley-and-hard-boiled-egg page sooner. At last the service began. I loved it when there was a typo and Evan read something really ridiculous without even realizing it. I tried not to laugh, but I couldn't stop the giggle that worked its way up from my toes, and when Jaimie and I looked at each other, we momentarily lost it altogether and were shushed.

Just as we got started again, Evan the Obnoxious spilled his grape juice down the front of my dress.

"Evan!" I squealed. "You ruined my dress!"

He didn't even say he was sorry. He just made an impolite noise with his mouth.

My mother jumped up to help me pat it dry, then wet it with water on a napkin. My stepgrandmother handed her the saltshaker.

Gregary the Gregarious was kicking at the folding table leg like he couldn't make his leg stop. Then the table collapsed and we all tried to catch the dishes and glasses inching down the tabletop.

"I'll help you clean up," I said to my stepgrandmother. None of the steps offered to help.

"It will be easier if I do it myself," she said.

"Thank you, Ariel," would have been nice, I thought to myself.

Soon both white linen tablecloths were covered with piles of salt that my stepgrandmother poured on each wine stain microseconds after it happened.

After that excitement, the littlest step recited the four questions in Hebrew and an older step translated them. Evan came up with a fifth question definitely meant to embarrass his mother.

"Why on this day do mothers wear dresses with a hole under the arm?" He was quickly sent away from the table, his mother racing after him.

Then we got to the part about the mortar and bricks and were busy with the haroset and matzah. That's when the littlest step got very impatient to open the door for the spirit of Elijah to enter and sip from the waiting silver cup of wine. Instead of at the end of the meal, she opened the door early and was almost blown over by the huge gust of cold wind that tore through the room.

I knew at once that this year the spirit of Elijah wasn't alone. . . . As everyone was trying to get the door closed and the younger steps were grabbing flying haggadahs, I thought I heard the first three notes to "Hot Cross Buns" on Grandma's piano even though nobody was near it. I smelled a slight whiff of Grandma's perfume, and my heart filled with happiness. Then as the door was shut with a last gust of wind, the place cards all flew around, and my card headed right to the seat next to my Grandpa. My Grandma's ghost took my hand. Her hand felt cold, but her finger had my grandmother's bump from writing a lot. She led me to the seat next to my grandfather, where Evan's mother had been sitting before the "incident." I laughed out loud and moved in to my new chair at the adults' table, just where I wanted to be.

"Hey, how come she gets to sit at the adult table?" Evan the Obnoxious yelled.

I pointed to my place card, which magically no longer said *Areel,* but *Ariel.*

Gregory the Gregarious said, "Not fair!"

And the littlest step just repeated what her brother said, only two times. "Not fair! Not fair!"

Grandpa said, "Let's take this problem step by step."

First he defended me. "You know Ariel always got to sit next to me when she was little. You know I love all of you, but since her place card flew over here, she has this seat. But I'll step over to the children's table and sit with all of you for dessert."

"Okay," Evan said, now sitting next to his mother at the children's table.

"Okay, that's fair," Gregory added.

"Okay, that's fair. Okay, that's fair," mimicked the littlest step.

So Grandpa and I yakked and yakked about school and hopes and dreams and sang "Ha Gadya" as fast as we could and hugged and whispered about Grandma.

"I still miss her a lot," I said.

"I do too," he answered. "We'll always love her, won't we?"

"Definitely," I said, and leaned my head on his shoulder. I think he also knew that her spirit was nearby.

Then we ate soup that smelled like soup and matzah balls with a hard spot in the middle like Grandma's, and everyone laughed and was happy.

"Maybe Grandma can watch over us and help more from wherever she is now?" I said to Grandpa.

"She'd be glad we're happy," Grandpa said.

After dinner, all us kids searched for the *afikoman,* the matzah that Grandpa had hidden at the beginning of the meal. Jaimie found it under a pillow, and Grandpa gave her a dollar. We all ate a piece of the matzah.

When the piano-banging problem started again, step-by-step I taught each one how to play "Hot Cross Buns" . . . gently. The littlest step had to play it twice. She said it sounded a little like "Ha Gadya." They were pretty good learners. And actually it was kind of fun. Jaimie joined me in a duet, and then my stepgrandmother clapped.

"Good job, kids," she said, and, "What a great teacher you are, Ariel."

"Thanks," I said.

It was a very special day. I looked around and smiled. There would be lots of new people to love, but I'd have my memories of my very special grandmother always. And I knew she'd watch over us.

As my grandmother's ghost got farther away, I felt warmth as my stepgrandmother said to me, "I can see you're having a good time, Ariel. I'm glad." I gave her a hug and meant it. And for the first time I shared something with her.

"Next year can I sit at the adult table with you and Grandpa?" I asked.

"Sure," she said, and she hugged me back.

~ Background Note from the Author ~

I know exactly when I decided to become a writer because I wrote it down. In my seventh-grade diary I wrote: "When I grow up I want to become a gernalist. I went to the library and got a pamflet on Gernalism for Boys." Spelling didn't count then; nor did not finding a book for girls.

I had a great time writing "My Grandma's Ghost" when I was asked by JPS to submit a short story for this anthology. I was very close to my own grandmothers, as were my children to theirs. My own grandchildren are so dear to me that I can imagine reaching out even from the great beyond to keep them safe and help them when needed. I still call on my own long-departed ancestors for strength. I've seen stories of stepfamilies, usually about siblings, but not about stepgrandparents and stepcousins, as is the case in so many of today's families. Drawing new members into a family without excluding memories of the past is not easy. I hope this story will help.

~ About the Author ~

CAROL SNYDER is the award-winning author of fourteen books for children from preschool to young adult, including *God Must Like Cookies, Too,* published by The Jewish Publication Society. Two of her *Ike and Mama* books have won the Association of Jewish Libraries and Sydney Taylor awards. Others have been American Booksellers Association Children's Pick of the Lists and *New York Times Book Review* selections. She is a member of the Children's Book Committee at Bank Street College of Education and serves on the Society of Children's Book Writers and Illustrators, New York Metro Chapter. She is now illustrating and exhibiting artwork as well as writing and lecturing in schools and libraries. She is married and lives in New York City. She is the proud mother of two daughters and has four grandchildren and a granddog.